# WINES & RECIPES

To my aunt Golla, who taught me
to cook in a delicious way

# WINES & RECIPES

Raul Diaz

# CONTENTS

# FOREWORDS

I have worked with Raul on many events, and to say it is a joy would be an understatement. Raul's passion for food and wine is infectious; he manages to captivate an audience with simple words that transport you to another world of pleasure.

This book is full of delicious recipes and wine recommendations guaranteed to ensure an unforgettable meal.

## — MICHEL ROUX JR

Raul Diaz is a well-recognised sommelier and wine educator and as such his role is to ensure that both diners and students get the most out of the wine in their glass. The sommelier aspect is the art of matching wine with food, while the teaching part is more a step-by-step approach to create better appreciation through knowledge. His book combines both in a disarming, almost simple way.

As someone whose mantra is 'drink for mood, not for food', wine and food pairing is not high on my list of priorities – though plainly I don't drink Barossa Shiraz with Whitstable oysters. But both wine and food have their origins, their unique 'sense of place', so when I open a Rioja my mind turns to northern Spain, and I know the bottle will drink well with whatever dishes my wife has prepared. One of the many strengths of this book is that Raul has matched the dish to the wine, both often coming from the same place and certainly complementing each other. Glancing through the recipes, I am transported to its home country and through his choice of wine I am already there, glass in hand, knives and forks at the ready.

In this busy world, wine and food remain one of the surest, most dependable pleasures that life has to offer. This book opens the door in a mouth-watering manner.

## — STEVEN SPURRIER

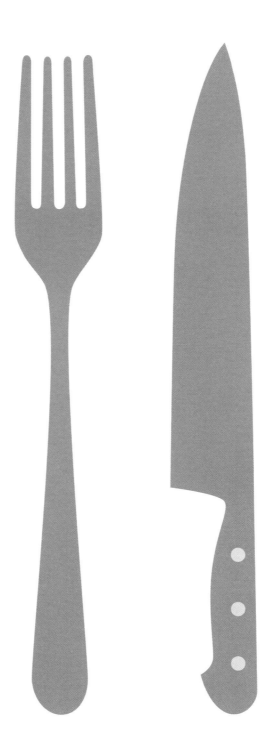

# INTRODUCTION

# WINES & RECIPES

The diversity of wine and food found throughout the world is astounding. When it comes to wine and food pairing, there are some basic 'rules' that can help guide us to successful matches. Understanding the interrelationship between wine and food helps to enhance our enjoyment of both. Ultimately you will develop your own personal preferences, but always, the goal remains the same: to enjoy a delicious glass of wine with a tasty dish. For me, I derive great pleasure from harmonious pairings. Each time I think about a particular wine, I dream a bit about its country of origin, the location of the vineyard and the people. Very quickly this leads to craving foods that pair well with that wine. A great combination can heighten the enjoyment of both the food and the wine.

My desire to share lesser-known grapes and wine styles (as well as some more familiar favourites) paired with delicious recipes was my inspiration for this book. This is not intended as a textbook or manual: it's a practical guide with information presented in a fun and straightforward manner, placing more emphasis on wine than on food. Although we all grow up eating food, we don't all grow up learning about wine. Here is an opportunity to learn about different wines and how best to pair them successfully with food.

This book isn't filled with rules. I won't tell you exactly what to do, nor will I give you strict guidelines about which food goes with which wine. Instead the book is filled with 50 pairings for you to try. It's a jumping-off point; one that will allow you to gain confidence and experience so that you can create your own pairing choices.

I am not a professional chef. I did, however, start cooking at a young age. Cooking nutritious and delicious food has been an essential part of my daily life for a long time. By profession I am a wine expert with more than 15 years' experience. I have spent much of my career tasting a wide variety of wines and pairing them with food.

I am very grateful for my Chilean roots. This book contains several classic recipes from Chile that I hope you will enjoy as much as I do. Although I was born in Chile, I have also lived in many other places. Throughout my career, I have had the privilege of travelling extensively, visiting over 100 countries. In each place I have visited, I have enjoyed soaking up the unique aromas and amazing flavours of the local cuisines. My cooking is a melding of my Chilean heritage and the influence of these diverse cultures. Over time, I have also become aware of the difference it makes to eat healthily. Consequently, it's important to me to create and share recipes that are good for you, in addition to being delicious.

It is not necessary to go through this book in order. Just pick a wine or a recipe that you fancy and go for it. You will find that, for the most part, the ingredients are easily accessible and that the recipes don't require complicated techniques. Nearly every recipe can be prepared in about 30–40 minutes. There are a few exceptions – I just couldn't resist including some of my absolute favourite recipes, such as Pastel de Choclo (page 119) or Parmigiana di Melanzane (page 67), even if they require a bit more preparation time.

The wine and food pairings in the book are there for your enjoyment and as guidelines. Don't be afraid to get creative and have fun experimenting with different combinations of your own choosing. Happy pairing!

— RAUL DIAZ

## ABOUT THE AUTHOR

Raul Diaz is a sommelier, founder of the Wine Training School in London and the UK Ambassador for VDP German wines. His modern approach to learning includes small classes with great student interaction. As well as teaching at his own school, he regularly teaches at the Wine & Spirits Education Trust. He hosts masterclasses for Taste of London, Imbibe Live, London Wine Fair, Wines of Chile and Wines of Spain. He is a wine collaborator for the food and drinks magazine *Foodism UK*.

For several years, Raul has been a wine presenter for the UK's Channel 4 television programme *Sunday Brunch*. In 2018, he received the Rioja Communicator of the Year award for his constant support in the promotion of Rioja wines.

For more information about wine courses, visit www.winetraining.co.uk
Instagram: @rauldiazwines

# WINE ESSENTIALS

**What is wine?** An alcoholic drink made from fermented grapes, wine has been made essentially the same way for thousands of years. And it all begins with the grapes.

## GRAPES

Wine grapes are not the same as table grapes – they tend to be smaller and sweeter. There are thousands of varieties, all with unique characteristics, and displaying an extraordinary range of acidity, colour, sweetness, aromas, flavours, tannins, body and finish. While wines are heavily impacted by the grape variety, other environmental factors, including the making process, influence the final style and quality.

## CLIMATE

Climate plays a huge role in the choice of grapes grown in a given area and the subsequent style of winemaking. The absence or abundance of sunshine and warmth will affect the finished wine. As grapes ripen, their sugar content increases. In a cool climate, the sugar in the grapes will be significantly lower due to the lack of warmth. Cool climate wines commonly have high levels of acidity, making them very refreshing to drink. White grape varieties, such as Riesling or Sauvignon Blanc, thrive in cooler climates.

In warm climates, the opposite is true. The sugar content of the grapes will be higher, resulting in riper fruit flavours and a lower level of acidity. Garnacha and Merlot are two black grapes that flourish in warmer climates.

You can really discern the difference that climate makes when comparing wines made from the same grape grown in different locations. For example, a Syrah produced in the Rhône Valley in France will have a very elegant structure with blackberry fruits and peppery notes. A Shiraz (the Australian name for Syrah) produced in the warmer Barossa Valley in Australia will showcase a richer body with riper blackberry fruits and sweet spice.

# TERROIR

Terroir comes from the Latin word 'terra' meaning land. It is an idea that expresses a wine's unique origin. A 'terroir' wine reflects a particular combination of many factors that are present in a specific place – not just climate, but also the soil, altitude, aspect, rainfall and many other variables.

Vineyards can be planted on flat terrain or on steep slopes. Slopes increase sun exposure and improve drainage and air ventilation, which are highly beneficial to grape crops, especially in challenging cool climate regions. Rivers can also increase the temperature in a vineyard by reflecting sunlight onto the slopes. In warmer climates, fog and cold winds can reduce vineyard temperatures allowing slow ripening of the grapes while maintaining high levels of acidity.

The soil in the vineyard also highly influences the wine's character, with the grapes, and subsequently the wine, often being an expression of the specific soil. Some soils, like granite, common to several wine regions such as the Beaujolais region and Rhône Valley, act as a heat retainer, reducing the impact of cool climates. Drainage is another important factor: some soils, like gravel, drain the water quickly while other soils, like clay, retain water. Higher water levels lead to bigger crops, reducing the concentration of flavours and sugars in the grapes. And nutrients in the soil impact the grapes, too: excessive growth can occur if a soil's nutrient levels are too high. Poor soil, with low amounts of nutrients, creates a smaller crop, which generally produces higher quality grapes.

Wine grapes will take up to six months to grow. When the winemaker is satisfied with the ripeness of the grape as measured by the levels of sugar, acid, and tannin, the grapes will be picked (harvested). The harvest period normally takes place between August and October in the northern hemisphere and February and April in the southern hemisphere. Depending on the vineyard specifics, such as flat terrain or steep slopes, harvests can be performed by machinery or by hand. Either method of harvesting can produce top quality wines. After picking, the grapes will be crushed in order to extract their juice.

# PROCESS

There are many techniques used to produce wines. Fermentation varies depending on the style. For white wine production, after crushing, the grapes will be pressed to extract all the remaining juice, separating it from the grape skins (although there are some exceptions to this rule – see Pinot Gris/Pinot Grigio profile on page 70). The juice is then transferred to a fermentation vessel – stainless-steel tanks, concrete vats or oak barrels – and yeast is added to start the fermentation.

# FERMENTATION

During fermentation, yeast will consume all (or almost all) of the sugar in the grapes and convert it to alcohol. Once this process is finished, the wine will mature for a certain period of time, depending on the style of wine being produced.

For red wine production, after crushing, the grapes will go directly to the fermentation vessel – normally a stainless-steel tank – along with the skins. Keeping the juice in contact with the skins means it picks up colour, aromas and tannins (natural preservatives that can be found on the stems and skins of the grapes allowing the wines to have a longer life). Once the red wine fermentation is completed, the grape skins are removed and discarded. The wine is then moved to a maturation vessel – stainless-steel tank, concrete vat or oak barrel – to mature based on the winemaker's choice. Oak – and in particular small new oak barrels – is very popular as it contains vanillin, which softens tannins in red wines and creates richer styles of wine with notes of toast, nuts, coconut or vanilla. Larger, older, oak barrels improve texture but rarely add to the aromas or flavours of the wine. Stainless steel tanks are very common maturation vessels that preserve the purity of the flavours. Maturation in new oak barrels adds elegant notes of toast, nuts and vanilla.

Rosé wines will have a short period of skin contact to get that beautiful pink colour and a little more flavour. Rosé wine fermentation is completed after the skins are removed.

The majority of wine goes through a single fermentation process, whereby yeast converts sugar into alcohol. As well as the initial alcoholic fermentation, most red wines – and many full-bodied whites – undergo a malolactic fermentation in the spring following the harvest in order to balance the acidity and increase drinkability. Sparkling wines often go through a secondary fermentation, creating bubbles (carbon dioxide or $CO_2$) and flavour complexity. Sparkling wine made with the 'traditional method' (where the secondary fermentation takes place inside the bottle – see page 200), such as champagne, will showcase incredible notes of yeast, bread and biscuit. Sparkling wine made with the 'tank method' (where the secondary fermentation takes place in a stainless-steel tank), for example Prosecco, will preserve the purity of the grape variety chosen.

# BLENDING

Blending is a winemaking technique that can have great influence over the final taste of a wine. Wines can be made from a single grape variety such as Chardonnay, Pinot Grigio or Pinot Noir. In other cases, the winemaker may blend two or more grape varieties together. For example, if someone refers to a red 'Bordeaux blend', they are talking about a combination of Cabernet Franc, Cabernet Sauvignon and Merlot. For Bordeaux reds the average fermentation time is 18 days. The fermentation time depends on different factors such as temperature, sugar level, the particular yeast that is used, desired alcoholic strength, and varies from one harvest to the next. Blending can add complexity, as each grape contributes different attributes to the wine. However, fermentation time may vary for different grape varieties – Cabernet Sauvignon often takes weeks, while Cabernet Franc may take only a few days. Therefore, blending takes place after each individual variety – each 'base wine' – has completed its fermentation. The Bordeaux blend for white wines is made from Semillon, Sauvignon Blanc and Muscadelle grapes.

# STORAGE & SERVING TEMPERATURE

There are a few key things you should keep in mind when it comes to storing your wine. It is very important to keep it at a constant temperature, ideally between 10$^\circ$C and 15$^\circ$C. Choose a location that is away from strong light and free of vibration. Bottles sealed with corks should always be stored on their side to keep the cork moist.

To get the most enjoyment out of your wine, it is important to serve it at the right temperature. Sparkling and dessert wines should always be well-chilled. Other white wines should be moderately chilled and most red wine should be closer to room temperature.

These are simple guidelines that will help to you to serve the wine at the perfect temperature, although throughout the book, I give serving temperature guidance for each wine.

**WELL CHILLED** (6–8$^\circ$C): Sparkling wines and sweet wines

**CHILLED** (7–10$^\circ$C): Light–medium bodied white and rosé wines

**LIGHTLY CHILLED** (12–13$^\circ$C): Medium–full bodied white wines and light bodied red wines

**ROOM TEMPERATURE** (15–18$^\circ$C): Medium–full bodied red wines

# GLASSWARE

There is no shortage of glassware available for wine. It has been proven that the shape of a wine glass has an effect on the taste of the wine. The most important features of a wine glass are its bowl shape and size, the slope of the sides and the size of the opening at the top.

A flute is the most common choice for a sparkling wine. It does a great job of preserving the bubbles in the wine.

Glasses for white wine tend to have smaller bowls and are more upright than red wine glasses. These help to concentrate the aromas and the smaller size allows wine to stay cool. This glass is also a great choice for rosé wines. It works well for many sparkling wines too!

Red wine glasses tend to be larger than white wine glasses with a round bowl that allows for air contact to reveal the more complex aromas of many red wines. A larger opening at the top of the glass allows for better detection of these aromas.

A dessert wine glass is appropriate for both dessert and fortified wines. These glasses are even smaller than white wine glasses because these wines tend to be higher in alcohol and therefore served in smaller amounts. This type of glass is designed to focus the wine from the centre back to the tip of your tongue for the most enjoyable detection of sweetness.

A decanter is a glass vessel used to hold wine. Decanting can be beneficial when drinking a complex and/or older wine – it is very popular for powerful red wines and fortified wines. Transferring the wine to a decanter introduces oxygen into the wine and can help make wines easier to drink, softening the perception of tannins and lowering the sensation of alcohol on your palate. Some wines, such as Vintage Port, can leave a sediment deposit as they age, and so decanting is also useful for extracting the wine from the bottle and leaving the sediment behind.

To decant, slowly pour the bottle of wine into a decanter. It is ideal to do this 45–60 minutes before drinking.

# TASTING WINE

If you want to taste wine like a pro, try following these steps: first, look at the appearance of the wine, then smell and finally taste the wine. When tasting, many people keep tasting notes so that they remember what they have tasted and are able to make a comparison with other wines they taste.

We can tell a lot about a wine from its appearance. Take a look at the wine in your glass. Hold your glass at a 45-degree angle using a clean white surface as a background. Look at its clarity. Is it clear or hazy? A hazy wine may be an indication of a problem. Next, how much colour does the wine have? We call this intensity and use the term 'pale' for a wine with little colour, 'deep' for one with a lot of colour and 'medium' for those that fall in the middle. There are standard terms that wine professionals use to discuss colour. For white wine: lemon, gold or amber, and for red wine: purple, ruby, garnet and tawny. The most common colour for white wine is lemon and for red wine, ruby.

After looking at its appearance, smell what's in your glass. We refer to this as the wine's 'nose'. First look for primary aromas.

These are aromas that come directly from the grapes. For white wines, examples include apple, melon, citrus fruits such as lemon and lime, stone fruits such as apricot and peach, and tropical fruits like lychee, pineapple and mango. In red wines, look for red and black fruits. The most common red fruits are cherry, strawberry and raspberry and for black fruits look for blackberry, blackcurrant, black plum and black cherry. Floral aromas like rose petals or chamomile and herbal aromas may also be present in either colour wine. Next look for secondary aromas. These are aromas that come as a result of post-fermentation winemaking techniques and include toast, vanilla and cream. Tertiary aromas are those that come from age. Look for things such as dried fruits, mushroom, leather, caramel and nutty flavours.

Now it's time to taste your wine. We call this the 'palate'. Take a generous sip of wine in your mouth and move it around before swallowing. Try to find the flavours you detected on the nose. Which ones are dominant? Are there any flavours or aromas that you smelt on the nose but don't taste on the palate?

Consider the body of the wine – the overall sensation in your palate of all the elements that a wine has – such as acidity, tannins, fruit flavours, oak notes (if they are present), and finish.

Finally, think about what you smelled and tasted. Do you like it? Do you judge it to be a good or great wine? If you're keeping notes, jot down some thoughts so you can more easily recall what you have tasted.

# WINE & FOOD MATCHING

When we eat food and drink wine together, the food has a notable effect on the way that we perceive the flavours in the wine. If we understand the general principles of this interaction, we can enhance our enjoyment of both the wine and food. There are some simple guidelines that will help you make some smart decisions about good pairings, but everyone has different sensitivities and preferences. It's best to understand these principles and then experiment and make decisions that suit you. Consider tasting wines without food, then pay attention to the changes that occur when you do eat something. It can be quite a revelation!

When we eat, our perception of things such as the saltiness or sweetness of a food are affected by what we have last tasted. A classic example – think about how unpleasant orange juice tastes right after brushing your teeth!

There are two characteristics in most of the dishes we eat that are very wine friendly: salt and acidity. When a food contains salt, we perceive the wine to be less bitter and acidic, more fruity and softer. The same is true for foods that are acidic. Additionally, many people find that pairing fatty, oily or fried food with wines with high acidity is very satisfying. The acidity in the wine gives the feeling of cleansing the palate by cutting through the oil. One of the most problematic food characteristics is sweetness. This will make a wine seem more bitter and acidic and will subdue the fruits. A good rule of thumb when pairing wine with something sweet is that the wine should be sweeter than the food, since the perceived level of sugar in the wine will be reduced by the sugar in the food.

Umami will have the same effect on wine as sweetness does. Umami is difficult to isolate because foods that are solely umami are rarely served on their own. Umami taste, which is a neutral and intense savouriness, is found in things such as walnuts, mushrooms and cured meats. The good news with umami is that adding salt helps to counteract the negative effects.

There are two other food characteristics to consider. A food that is highly flavoured generally works best with wine with equal flavour intensity. If the wine is too delicate, it will be overwhelmed by the taste of the food. Likewise, a delicate dish can be overpowered by an intensely flavoured wine. You should also be aware of chilli heat and its interaction with wine. The intensity of the heat or burning sensation felt when eating chillies can vary greatly depending upon the individual. Some people actually enjoy this sensation while others do not. Alcohol in wine increases this sensation – the higher the alcohol in the wine drank alongside, the more intense the sensation of heat in the food. Knowing this, you can decide for yourself how you want your wine to interact with the heat from chillies in a dish.

# PANTRY

There are some basic ingredients that appear in quite a few of the recipes in this book. It will make your life easier to have them ready in your pantry.

• Capers
• Couscous
• Bay leaves
• Black pepper
• Dijon mustard
• Dried chilli flakes

- Dried spaghetti
- Eggs
- Garlic
- Ginger
- Greek yoghurt
- Honey
- Lemons
- Limes
- Olive oil
- Onions (red and white)
- Paprika
- Parmesan
- Plain flour
- Pita bread
- Rice: long grain, basmati and Thai jasmine
- Sea salt
- Sunflower oil
- Tinned tomatoes

# HOW TO USE THIS BOOK

This book is a practical guide to wine and food pairing. I have organised it so that each grape (or in some cases wine style) is paired with a recipe – for example, a Sauvignon Blanc makes the perfect pairing with a Ceviche (see page 79). The grape or wine profile faces the recipe, providing you with all the relevant wine information alongside the instructions for preparing the dish.

I have kept the structure of the wine profiles simple and relevant. Each one has key information about the grape or wine style. You can see the country of origin, other countries where the wine is grown, the main regions and famous appellations. All criteria are organised alphabetically.

The following pages showcase 41 grape varieties and 9 wine styles – this is because, while you can recognise wines by the grape variety anywhere in the world, in Europe the appellation systems (specifically defined areas for growing grapes and making wine) mean that wines are often named by their region, rather than by grape variety. These specific denominations of origin have strict rules governing the grape variety that can be used, the maximum yield, the use of oak treatment, etc. For example, a region of origin such as Côte de Beaune will lend its name to the wine rather than the Chardonnay (for white wine) or Pinot Noir (for red wine) grapes that the wine is made from.

Either way, the profiles provide pertinent details such as: the 'home country' of the grape – where it originated or which country has built a reputation as the main country for that grape; which region or appellation the wine is from; or how much you could expect to pay for a wine. The 'tasting notes' section gives an indication of what to expect from a wine made from a certain grape: levels of sweetness, acidity and alcohol. Fruits are evaluated giving an indication as to how delicate or intense the aromas and flavours are. Body, the sensation of how a wine feels in the mouth, is also rated from light to full-bodied.

For your reference, there is also a glossary of wine terms at the back of the book, in case any unfamiliar terms come up.

# SPARKLING WINE

# CAVA

**HOME COUNTRY: SPAIN**
—

**MAIN REGIONS: NAVARRA,
PENEDÈS, RIOJA AND
VALENCIA**
—

**FAMOUS APPELLATIONS:
CAVA**
—

**SWEETNESS: DRY TO SWEET**
—

**FRUITS: MEDIUM**
—

**ACIDITY: MEDIUM TO HIGH**
—

**ALCOHOL: MEDIUM**
—

**BODY: LIGHT**
—

**GLASSWARE: FLUTE
AND WHITE**
—

**TEMPERATURE:
WELL CHILLED**
—

**CELLAR: DRINK AS SOON
AS POSSIBLE UNLESS
YOU HAVE A CAVA GRAN
RESERVA THAT CAN AGE
REALLY WELL, FROM 5–10
YEARS.**
—

**BUDGET: £–££**

Cava is a flavourful sparkling wine made using a blend of three Spanish grapes and vinified using the traditional method. This method, originating from the Champagne region in France (see page 28), gives the wine its characteristic yeasty and bready notes. The appellation of Cava is unusual in that it can be produced in several different regions around Spain. However, the region of Catalunya, where Penedès is located, accounts for more than 97 per cent of national production. The majority of cava produced is non-vintage and is best consumed within a few years of release. Non-vintage cava is made from a blend of wines that were made from grapes that were picked in different years. Vintage cava is made only with grapes from a single harvest. This wine has a long ageing potential.

**GRAPES:**
The three grapes of cava bring different things to the blend. Macabeo contributes high acidity and lovely stone fruits. Xarel-lo adds body and alcohol. Parellada has fresh citrus fruits to round out the blend.

**STYLES:**
'Basic' cava is generally the house style and by law must be aged for a minimum of nine months prior to release. With Cava Reserva the ageing requirement increases to a minimum of 15 months; expect great quality and a more complex wine. Gran Reserva is the best quality of the three styles and must be aged for no less than 30 months. Cava de Paraje Calificado is the latest classification that applies to cava produced using high-quality grapes from a specific place (Paraje). This is a vintage cava with a minimum ageing period of 36 months.

**FLAVOURS:**
Lemon, lime, apple, pear, apricot, bread, biscuit, yeast

# PAN CON TOMATE
## [GRILLED BREAD WITH TOMATOES]

**SERVES: 4**

---

**TIME: 15 MINS**

---

**VEGETARIAN**

---

4 large, ripe tomatoes
1 tbsp extra virgin olive oil, plus extra to serve
1 tsp sea salt, plus extra to serve
4 thick slices of sourdough bread
1 garlic clove

*Pan con tomate* is a fantastic recipe to enjoy with your friends and family. It's easy, quick and delicious. When working with fresh ingredients, dishes can be simple and still have a lot of punch. The acidity of tomatoes is a difficult one to match, but **Cava**'s crisp and yeasty nature makes it a good pairing. This is perfect for aperitif time!

1. Cut the tomatoes in half. Holding them by the uncut side, grate them into a small bowl using the smallest holes on a grater, leaving behind the stems and skins. Add the olive oil and salt to the tomato pulp.

2. Toast slices of bread in the toaster or on a griddle pan until nicely charred.

3. Cut the garlic clove in half, then rub the cut side on the toasted bread. Don't skip this step – it adds needed flavour to the bread.

4. Spread the tomato paste onto the slices of bread, drizzle over a little more olive oil and add a final scattering of salt to taste.

'The acidity of tomatoes is a difficult one to match, but Cava's crisp and yeasty nature makes it a good pairing'

CAVA WITH PAN CON TOMATE

# CHAMPAGNE

**HOME COUNTRY: FRANCE**

**MAIN REGIONS: CHAMPAGNE**

**FAMOUS APPELLATIONS: CHAMPAGNE**

**SWEETNESS: DRY TO SWEET**

**FRUITS: MEDIUM**

**ACIDITY: HIGH**

**ALCOHOL: MEDIUM**

**BODY: LIGHT**

**GLASSWARE: FLUTE AND WHITE**

**TEMPERATURE: WELL CHILLED**

**CELLAR: NON-VINTAGE ARE READY TO DRINK. VINTAGE CHAMPAGNE CAN AGE REALLY WELL FOR 10–15+ YEARS.**

**BUDGET: £££**

Champagne gets its sparkle by undergoing a second fermentation (see page 200 for the stages involved in what is called the traditional method). This fermentation takes place in the bottle, creating carbon dioxide and a unique flavour profile. Even after the second fermentation has finished, the bottles rest in chalk caves for a period of time while the unique bread and yeast flavours develop. In Champagne, the law requires that all grapes must be hand-picked to ensure that only the best-quality fruit is used. In general, champagne is a mix of many still wines that are blended together to make the finished sparkling wine.

**GRAPES:**
There are three main grapes that can be used to produce champagne: one white and two black. Chardonnay, the white grape, has high acidity and citrus fruits that it contributes to a blend. Pinot Noir, the main black grape, lends red fruit character and body. The second black grape, Pinot Meunier, contributes body and texture and is normally used in relatively small amounts.

**STYLES:**
The majority of wines are non-vintage and generally express the champagne house style. They are required to be aged for a minimum of 15 months. Blanc de Blancs must be made using 100 per cent Chardonnay grapes. Blanc de Noirs requires the inclusion of only the black grapes, Pinot Noir and/or Meunier. Rosé Champagne is made with the addition of a small amount of red wine (normally from Pinot Noir) during the blending process. Vintage Champagne is not made every year; it is made only in the best years and reflects the conditions of that specific year rather than the house style. It is required to be aged for a minimum of 36 months.

**FLAVOURS:**
Lemon, lime, green apple, apricot, cherry, bread, biscuit, nuts, toast

# PRAWN & MANGO SALAD

**SERVES: 2**

———

**TIME: 20 MINS**

———

120g rocket
1 mango, peeled, pitted
    and sliced
250g cherry tomatoes, halved
1 avocado, peeled, pitted and
    chopped into large dice
2 tbsp extra virgin olive oil
1 garlic clove, sliced
200g large raw prawns, peeled
juice of 1 lemon
a small bunch of coriander,
    chopped
sea salt and black pepper

Too often people save **Champagne** for a special occasion, thinking that it needs to be paired with something special and fussy to prepare. Instead, I like to match Champagne with this lovely, simple prawn salad. The acidity of the lemon juice in the salad amplifies the fruit flavours in the wine – and the prawns hold up well with Champagne's high acidity.

1. Spread the rocket over a serving plate large enough to accommodate the finished salad. Arrange the mango, cherry tomatoes and avocado on top, and season to taste.

2. Heat a frying pan over a medium heat and add the olive oil and garlic. When the garlic starts to turn golden, remove it from the pan and discard.

3. Add the prawns to the pan and cook for 3–4 minutes, turning once, until pink and opaque. Season with salt and pepper. Add the lemon juice and the coriander to the pan and cook for another 1 minute.

4. Add the warm prawns to the serving plate and drizzle over all the lemony juices from the pan. Toss all the ingredients together and serve immediately.

'The acidity of the lemon juice in the salad amplifies the fruit flavours in the wine'

CHAMPAGNE WITH PRAWN & MANGO SALAD

# PROSECCO

**HOME COUNTRY: ITALY**

---

**MAIN REGIONS:**
**FRIULI AND VENETO**

---

**FAMOUS APPELLATIONS:**
**CONEGLIANO**
**VALDOBBIADENE PROSECCO**
**SUPERIORE AND PROSECCO**

---

**SWEETNESS: DRY**
**AND OFF-DRY**

---

**FRUITS: MEDIUM**

---

**ACIDITY: MEDIUM TO HIGH**

---

**ALCOHOL: MEDIUM**

---

**BODY: LIGHT**

---

**GLASSWARE: FLUTE**
**AND WHITE**

---

**TEMPERATURE:**
**WELL CHILLED**

---

**CELLAR: 1–2 YEARS**

---

**BUDGET: £–££**

Prosecco is the name of a sparkling white wine from the Friuli-Venezia Giulia and Veneto regions of northeast Italy. Unlike cava and champagne, prosecco is not produced using the traditional method, where secondary fermentation occurs in the bottle. Rather, the sparkle is produced in a large tank in a process unsurprisingly called the tank method. It is an excellent way to produce sparkling wines made from aromatic grape varieties as it preserves the flavours and freshness of the grapes. For the most part, these wines should be consumed shortly after release as they don't have much potential for ageing. The hillside terroir appellation of Conegliano Valdobbiadene Prosecco Superiore is responsible for the highest quality expression of Prosecco in Italy.

**GRAPES:**
Glera is an ancient variety from the regions of Friuli-Venezia Giulia and Veneto. This grape produces wines with medium to high acidity and intense aromas of peach, pear and very elegant floral notes.

**STYLES:**
There are two different styles of prosecco produced: Frizzante is lightly sparkling, whereas Spumante is fully sparkling.

**FLAVOURS:**
Lemon, lime, peach, apricot, melon, floral notes

# CHILEAN BRUSCHETTA

**SERVES: 4**

——

**TIME: 15 MINS**

——

**VEGETARIAN**

——

2 avocados, peeled and pitted
1 tbsp extra virgin olive oil,
　plus a drizzle to serve
4 slices sourdough or crusty
　white bread
a handful of cherry tomatoes,
　halved
½ bunch of coriander, finely
　chopped
sea salt

A typical breakfast in Chile is toasted bread spread with what the locals call '*palta*' – avocado purée. My take on this Chilean classic includes a few extra ingredients. No need to eat this only for breakfast, it makes a wonderful and filling snack at any time of day. The floral character and acidity of **Prosecco** make it a natural pairing with this bruschetta.

1. Put the avocado in a bowl and smash with a fork until you have a purée. Add the olive oil and season to taste with salt.

2. Toast the slices of bread, then divide the avocado purée between the slices and spread. Place a few tomato halves on top of each toast and scatter over the coriander. Add an extra drizzle of olive oil and a sprinkle of sea salt and serve.

# WHITE WINE

# ALVARINHO
# [ALBARIÑO]

**HOME COUNTRY: PORTUGAL**
—

**OTHER COUNTRIES: SPAIN**
—

**MAIN REGIONS: GALICIA, MELGAÇO, MINHO, MONÇÃO**
—

**FAMOUS APPELLATIONS: RÍAS BAIXAS, VINHO VERDE**
—

**SWEETNESS: DRY**
—

**FRUITS: HIGH**
—

**ACIDITY: HIGH**
—

**ALCOHOL: MEDIUM**
—

**BODY: MEDIUM**
—

**GLASSWARE: WHITE**
—

**TEMPERATURE: WELL CHILLED**
—

**CELLAR: 2–3 YEARS**
—

**BUDGET: ££**

Alvarinho (Albariño in Spanish) is an extremely aromatic grape variety brimming with stone and citrus fruit aromas. The flavours are similar to those found in Gewurztraminer or Viognier, but Alvarinho has much higher acidity. It is not unusual to find tiny bubbles in some of the wines made with Alvarinho. It is the key grape in Portugese Vinho Verde.

**STYLES:**
Alvarinho is frequently found as a varietal. This crisp wine displays zesty citrus and softer stone fruits with a briny minerality. In the region of Vinho Verde in the north of Portugal – one of the most popular appellations for white wine in the country – Alvarinho can make up 100 per cent of the wine. However, it is also blended with Loureiro and potentially a few other local grapes such as Arinto, Avesso, Azal and Trajadura to create delicious white wines.

**FLAVOURS:**
Lemon, lime, grapefruit, apple, apricot, peach, mango, floral notes

# COD, ASPARAGUS, TOMATOES & TOASTED ALMONDS

**SERVES: 2**

———

**TIME: 25 MINS**

———

50g flaked almonds
a bunch of asparagus, trimmed
2 tbsp extra virgin olive oil,
   plus extra for drizzling
250g cherry tomatoes
2 cod fillets
a squeeze of lemon juice
sea salt and black pepper

Cod is a favourite fish of mine; it has great flavour and texture. The right vegetables enhance the flavours of the fish without overpowering it, so find the balance and the dish will be magical. I fondly remember eating something similar to this and sipping a crisp, chilled glass of **Alvarinho** while watching the boats at the port of Lisbon. You may not be able to visit Lisbon right now, but you can enjoy this amazing combination in your own home.

1. Heat a pan over a medium heat, add the flaked almonds and toast for 2–3 minutes until golden and smelling good. Remove them from the pan and set aside.

2. Bring a saucepan of water to the boil. Add the asparagus and blanch for 2 minutes, then drain and run under cold water.

3. Heat a frying pan over a medium heat and add 1 tablespoon of the olive oil. Add the tomatoes, asparagus and a pinch of salt and sauté the vegetables for 4–5 minutes, stirring occasionally, until charred and softened. Remove the pan from the heat.

4. At the same time in another frying pan heat another 1 tablespoon of olive oil. Season the cod with salt and pepper and cook, skin side down, for about 3–4 minutes until the skin is golden and crisp and the fish almost cooked through. Flip the fish and cook for an additional 1–2 minutes until the fish is cooked through and just opaque.

5. Arrange the asparagus and the tomatoes on a platter or on individual plates and place the cooked cod on top. Squeeze over a little lemon juice, add a drizzle of olive oil and another pinch of sea salt. Scatter the toasted almonds around the fish and serve.

'Alvarinho is an extremely aromatic grape variety brimming with stone and citrus fruit aromas'

ALVARINHO WITH COD, ASPARAGUS, TOMATOES & TOASTED ALMONDS

# ASSYRTIKO

**HOME COUNTRY: GREECE**

---

**OTHER COUNTRIES:
MACEDONIA**

---

**MAIN REGIONS: PAROS,
PELOPONNESE, SANTORINI**

---

**FAMOUS APPELLATIONS:
SANTORINI, SLOPES OF
MELITON, VINSANTO**

---

**SWEETNESS: DRY TO SWEET**

---

**FRUITS: MEDIUM**

---

**ACIDITY: HIGH**

---

**ALCOHOL: HIGH**

---

**BODY: MEDIUM TO FULL**

---

**GLASSWARE: WHITE**

---

**TEMPERATURE:
WELL CHILLED**

---

**CELLAR: 5–10 YEARS**

---

**BUDGET: £–££**

Wines made from Assyrtiko are a bit unusual but are extremely elegant. This white grape calls the island of Santorini home, but it is now grown throughout Greece, where it is one of the most notable indigenous grapes. Expect a lean white wine possessing good minerality, texture and density.

**STYLES:**
When unoaked, these wines have high acidity with aromas of citrus and stone fruits dominating. Richer styles are produced when barrel aged, adding toasty notes and tropical fruits to the wine. A sweet version, called Vinsanto, is made using Assyrtiko grapes that were dried in the sun after harvest prior to vinification.

**FLAVOURS:**
Lemon, lime, herbs, passion fruit, salt

# GREEK SALAD

**SERVES: 4**

—

**TIME: 15 MINS**

—

**VEGETARIAN**

8 tomatoes (try to get a
    variety of shapes and sizes),
    cut into irregular wedges
2 cucumbers, roughly
    chopped
1 red onion, very thinly sliced
200g Kalamata olives, pitted
    and torn
1 tbsp dried oregano
juice of 1 lemon
4–5 tbsp extra virgin olive oil
200g feta, crumbled
sea salt and black pepper
warm pita bread, to serve

FOR THE TZATZIKI:
1 cucumber
400g Greek yoghurt
1 garlic clove, crushed
juice of 1 lemon
a bunch of fresh mint, leaves
    finely chopped
1 tbsp extra virgin olive oil

Nowadays, we all seem to have busy schedules and can find it challenging to cook meals that are healthy and appealing. When we find ourselves craving something nourishing and nutritious but are short on time, this salad is the perfect solution. **Assyrtiko**, the signature white grape variety of Greece, pairs well. Its texture is fantastic and especially complements the feta, Kalamata olives and fresh tomatoes in the salad.

1. Add the tomatoes, cucumbers, onion and olives to a bowl or platter. Scatter over the oregano, and drizzle with the lemon juice and olivè oil. Season well and gently toss to combine.

2. Add the crumbled feta to the salad.

3. To make the tzatziki, grate the cucumber, then use your hands to squeeze out any excess water.

4. Combine the cucumber, yoghurt, garlic, lemon juice and a good handful of the chopped fresh mint leaves. Add the olive oil and season with salt and black pepper to taste.

5. Serve the salad with warm pita bread and the tzatziki.

'Assyrtiko is one of the most notable indigenous grapes of Greece'

ASSYRTIKO & GREEK SALAD

# CHARDONNAY

**HOME COUNTRY: FRANCE**
—

**OTHER COUNTRIES:
AUSTRALIA, CHILE, NEW
ZEALAND, SOUTH AFRICA, USA**
—

**MAIN REGIONS: BURGUNDY,
MARGARET RIVER, NAPA
VALLEY**
—

**FAMOUS APPELLATIONS:
CHABLIS, CHASSAGNE-
MONTRACHET, MEURSAULT,
PULIGNY-MONTRACHET**
—

**SWEETNESS: DRY**
—

**FRUITS: LOW TO HIGH**
—

**ACIDITY: MEDIUM TO HIGH**
—

**ALCOHOL: MEDIUM TO HIGH**
—

**BODY: LIGHT TO FULL**
—

**GLASSWARE: WHITE**
—

**TEMPERATURE: CHILLED**
—

**CELLAR: YOUNG EXAMPLES
SHOULD BE CONSUMED
SOON (2–3 YEARS). TOP
BURGUNDIAN WINES CAN
AGE FOR 15–20+ YEARS.**
—

**BUDGET: £–£££**

Throughout the world, Chardonnay is one of the most widely planted and most successful white grape varieties. A big reason for its success is its adaptability. Chardonnay has the ability to flourish in nearly all climates suitable for vines. Not only does the character of the wine change with climate, but it also expresses differently with varying terroir. Winemaking techniques can also play a major role in the taste of the finished wine.

**STYLES:**
When unoaked, the wines range from those that are light bodied, high in acidity and predominantly display citrus fruits to those with fuller body, less acidity and stone/tropical fruit flavours. With the introduction of oak, expect a more complex, rich wine with hints of butter and/or cream. These wines still have good acidity and are more likely to have tropical fruit flavours. Chardonnay is a major component of many sparkling wines, including those from the region of Champagne.

**FLAVOURS:**
Lemon, lime, peach, apricot, mango, pineapple, butter, toast, nuts, coconut, vanilla

# GRILLED SARDINES WITH PEBRE

**SERVES: 4**

———

**TIME: 20 MINS**

———

16 sardines, cleaned and
    gutted
olive oil, for greasing
2 lemons, cut into wedges
a bunch of parsley, finely
    chopped
slices of toasted ciabatta,
    to serve

FOR THE PEBRE:
4 tomatoes, deseeded and
    very finely chopped
1 garlic clove, crushed
juice of ½ lemon
a small bunch of coriander,
    finely chopped
½ red onion, very finely
    chopped
1 large red chilli, deseeded
    and very finely chopped
5 tbsp extra virgin olive oil
sea salt and black pepper

Sardines may be quite humble, but they are packed with an intense flavour and a satisfying oily texture. Keeping this recipe simple allows them to showcase their assets. *Pebre* is a spicy tomato salsa that comes from my homeland of Chile. Eat this classic dish with a glass of chilled **Chardonnay**. For fun, given that there are so many different expressions of Chardonnay, make this recipe often and experiment with the many styles from different parts of the world to find the one you enjoy the most.

1. First, make the pebre by combining all the ingredients in a bowl. Season with salt and pepper and set aside.

2. Wash the sardines under running water to clean them inside and out and to remove any scales. Dry them well with kitchen paper.

3. Preheat the grill to very hot and oil a grill tray. Place the sardines on the tray, brush them with the pebre sauce on both sides, season with salt and put them under the grill. Cook for around 3–4 minutes on each side until cooked through and nicely charred.

4. Transfer the sardines to a serving plate and squeeze plenty of lemon juice over them. Scatter with the parsley and serve with the remaining lemon wedges and leftover *pebre*, as well as toasted slices of ciabatta alongside.

# CHENIN BLANC

**HOME COUNTRY: FRANCE**

**OTHER COUNTRIES: SOUTH AFRICA, USA**

**MAIN REGIONS: LANGUEDOC-ROUSILLON, LOIRE, NAPA VALLEY, PAARL**

**FAMOUS APPELLATIONS: ANJOU, COTEAUX DU LAYON, SAUMUR, SAVENNIÈRES, VOUVRAY**

**SWEETNESS: DRY TO SWEET**

**FRUITS: LOW TO HIGH**

**ACIDITY: MEDIUM TO HIGH**

**ALCOHOL: MEDIUM**

**BODY: LIGHT TO FULL**

**GLASSWARE: WHITE**

**TEMPERATURE: CHILLED**

**CELLAR: 3 YEARS FOR YOUNG WINES, COMPLEX SWEET WINES CAN AGE FOR 10+ YEARS**

**BUDGET: £–££**

Chenin Blanc is a grape that has been grown in the Loire Valley in northern France for at least a thousand years. This versatile grape produces a range of styles, from dry to sweet and also sparkling. The dry wines are refreshing thanks to the grape's natural high acidity. This acidity also allows the grapes to be affected by noble rot, and so they can be successfully vinified as a delicious sweet wine. Chenin Blanc wines can be drunk young but also have the ability to improve with age and gain complexity.

**STYLES:**
Unoaked wines are found in the Loire Valley and are crisp and light in style. Oaked wines from South Africa are richer and more complex with tropical flavours. Sweet wines, made from botrytised (nobly rotted) grapes, have concentrated flavours. Especially notable are the sweet wines from Vouvray and Coteaux du Layon.

**FLAVOURS:**
Lemon, apple, pear, peach, mango, banana, honey, marzipan

# BEETROOT, FETA & WALNUT SALAD

**SERVES: 4**

——

**TIME: 15 MINS**

——

**VEGETARIAN**

——

FOR THE SALAD:
180g lamb's lettuce
250g cooked beetroot
200g feta, crumbled
½ bunch of spring onions,
    finely chopped
a bunch of mint, leaves picked
100g walnuts, toasted and
    crushed

FOR THE DRESSING:
3 tbsp extra virgin olive oil
3 tbsp lemon juice
1 tbsp honey
1 heaped tsp Dijon mustard

It seems to me that beetroot is underrated as a main ingredient. This vegetable possesses natural sweetness and a texture that delivers a delightful sensation in your mouth. **Chenin Blanc** is a grape that produces rich and fruity wines with great intensity. It will match perfectly with this delicate and delectable recipe. Once you've tried this simple recipe, you'll never ignore beets again!

1.  Place the lamb's lettuce in a large bowl or spread over a platter.

2.  Cut the beetroot into wedges and arrange them on top of the lamb's lettuce.

3.  Sprinkle over the feta, spring onions, mint leaves and walnuts.

4.  For the dressing, whisk all the ingredients together.

5.  Drizzle the dressing over the salad and lightly toss to combine.

'Chenin Blanc is a grape that produces rich and fruity wines with great intensity'

CHENIN BLANC WITH BEETROOT, FETA & WALNUT SALAD

# GARGANEGA

**HOME COUNTRY: ITALY**

**MAIN REGIONS: FRIULI, UMBRIA, VENETO**

**FAMOUS APPELLATIONS: BIANCO DI CUSTOZA, COLLI BERICI, COLLI EUGANEI, GAMBELLARA, SOAVE**

**SWEETNESS: DRY AND SWEET**

**FRUITS: MEDIUM TO HIGH**

**ACIDITY: HIGH**

**ALCOHOL: MEDIUM**

**BODY: LIGHT FO FULL**

**GLASSWARE: WHITE**

**TEMPERATURE: WELL CHILLED**

**CELLAR: 3 YEARS FOR DRY WINES. 10+ YEARS FOR SWEET WINES.**

**BUDGET: ££**

Garganega is an ancient grape that has been cultivated in Veneto since as early as the 6th century. This grape grows vigorously and ripens late. When made well, Garganega produces a delicate wine with citrus fruits, good acidity and nice texture. Top wines come from the vineyards on the steep slopes within the designated Soave Classico area of Veneto. In Italian wine terms, Classico always indicates the grapes have come from the best (and generally the oldest) vineyards, where the vines are located on slopes and are close to the historic centre of the appellation.

**STYLES:**
When young, the wines are easy to drink, showing citrus fruit and hints of white peach. If the grapes come from the sloped vineyards, expect a more complex, rich style. In addition to riper fruits, these wines will also have notes of almonds and honey. These better wines can also age beautifully, adding even more complexity. Tasting of tropical fruits and sweet spices, Recioto di Soave, made from dried grapes, is a complex sweet wine.

**FLAVOURS:**
Apple, pear, chamomile, white peach, almond, nut, honey

# SPAGHETTI ALLA PUTTANESCA

**SERVES: 4**

——

**TIME: 15 MINS**

——

1 tbsp olive oil
1 onion, finely chopped
1 garlic clove, crushed
½ tsp dried chilli flakes
6 anchovies, chopped
20 black olives, pitted
2 tbsp capers, drained
    and rinsed
1 x 400g tin chopped
    tomatoes
400g spaghetti
a small bunch of basil,
    roughly chopped
freshly grated Parmesan,
    to serve
sea salt and black pepper

What if you're at home, it's dinnertime and you don't have a lot of things in your fridge? *Spaghetti alla puttanesca* is an option that requires just a handful of things that you're likely to have stocked in your kitchen. To pair with it, find a Soave from a good producer. The **Garganega** grape is a pleaser with its refreshing acidity, stone fruit character and floral aromas.

1. Heat the oil in a large frying pan over a medium heat and fry the onion for about 8–10 minutes until beginning to soften.

2. Add the garlic and chilli flakes and cook for another 1 minute. Add the anchovies, olives and capers and cook for 1 minute until the anchovies have dissolved.

3. Add the tomatoes and allow to simmer and reduce while you cook the pasta according to the instructions on the pack. To finish the sauce, season with salt and pepper and add the basil.

4. When the pasta is al dente, add it to the tomato sauce along with a cup of the pasta cooking water. Mix all ingredients well, then serve with plenty of freshly grated Parmesan.

# GEWURZTRAMINER

**HOME COUNTRY: FRANCE**

**OTHER COUNTRIES: AUSTRALIA, AUSTRIA, GERMANY, ITALY, NEW ZEALAND, USA**

**MAIN REGIONS: ALSACE, ALTO ADIGE, BADEN, PFALZ**

**FAMOUS APPELLATIONS: ALSACE, ALTO ADIGE, BADEN, PFALZ**

**SWEETNESS: DRY TO SWEET**

**FRUITS: HIGH**

**ACIDITY: LOW**

**ALCOHOL: HIGH**

**BODY: FULL**

**GLASSWARE: WHITE**

**TEMPERATURE: CHILLED**

**CELLAR: 2–3 YEARS**

**BUDGET: ££**

The homeland of Gewurztraminer is the region of Alsace in France. This grape is also found in several regions around the world such as Alto Adige, Burgenland, Pfalz, Victoria and others. Gewurztraminer is a difficult grape to grow successfully as it is very particular about its soil and climate. When grown under the right conditions, this grape has the unique perfumed quality of honey and rose petals, which is sublime. But, if the grape is harvested under-ripe or is over-cropped, it makes for an uninteresting wine. As it is naturally low in acidity, Gewurztraminer is best consumed in the first few years after release, when it is still crisp and the aromas are at their best.

**STYLES:**
Dry Gewurztraminer is a perfumed and full-bodied wine. With a touch of residual sugar, off-dry wines have added texture and richness that are balanced by delicious tropical fruits. Fabulous examples of sweet Gewurztraminer are made in Alsace: Vendange Tardive wines are made from grapes that are late harvested (as the name in French indicates) and Sélection de Grains Nobles are made from botrytised grapes (the noble rot).

**FLAVOURS:**
Lime, orange, lychee, mango, pineapple, rose petals, honey

# SPICY SQUID, TOMATOES & PARSLEY

**SERVES: 2**

———

**TIME: 25 MINS**

———

3 tbsp extra virgin olive oil
2 garlic cloves, sliced
250g cherry tomatoes, halved
1 tbsp sweet smoked paprika
1 fresh chilli, finely chopped
2 baby squid, cleaned and
    cut into rings
a bunch of parsley, finely
    chopped
juice of 1 lemon
sea salt and black pepper
baguette or sourdough,
    toasted, to serve

I love to drink **Gewurztraminer** with a wide variety of dishes. This full-bodied wine has great aromas, vibrant fruit flavours and a hint of spice. With its intense flavours, it requires a dish with equal intensity and interest. Spicy squid with fresh tomatoes and aromatic parsley is a great option.

1. Heat a frying pan over a medium heat and add the olive oil and the garlic. Once the garlic turns golden, remove from the pan and discard. Add the tomatoes to the garlicky oil and cook for around 5 minutes until the tomatoes begin to break down and release their juice.

2. Add the paprika and chilli and cook for another 1 minute. Add the squid and cook, stirring, for 3 minutes, or until it is opaque. Add the parsley and lemon juice and season with salt and pepper.

3. Serve immediately with toasted bread.

'When grown under the right conditions, Gewurztraminer has the unique perfumed quality of honey and rose petals – sublime'

GEWURZTRAMINER WITH SPICY SQUID, TOMATOES & PARSLEY

# GODELLO

**HOME COUNTRY: SPAIN**

—

**OTHER COUNTRIES: PORTUGAL**

—

**MAIN REGIONS: DOURO, GALICIA, VALDEORRAS**

—

**FAMOUS APPELLATIONS: BIERZO, RIBEIRA SACRA, VALDEORRAS**

—

**SWEETNESS: DRY**

—

**FRUITS: MEDIUM TO HIGH**

—

**ACIDITY: MEDIUM TO HIGH**

—

**ALCOHOL: MEDIUM**

—

**BODY: MEDIUM**

—

**GLASSWARE: WHITE**

—

**TEMPERATURE: WELL CHILLED**

—

**CELLAR: 2 YEARS**

—

**BUDGET: ££**

This dynamic Galician white grape was almost wiped out by the devastation caused by phylloxera at the end of the 1800s. Godello is an aromatic grape that stands up well on its own but also blends successfully with other varieties. Its refreshing acidity and pronounced minerality are paired with citrus and green fruit flavours and some floral notes. Wines can also develop depth in texture and flavour with the introduction of oak. It is one of the most exciting white grape varieties due to its adaptability and aromatic profile.

**STYLES:**
When unoaked, these incredibly aromatic wines remain clean and crisp. With the addition of time in oak, the wines become richer and generally have even more texture.

**FLAVOURS:**
Lemon, lime, pear, peach, mango, floral notes

# GAZPACHO

**SERVES: 4**

---

**TIME: 20 MINS**

---

**VEGETARIAN**

---

1kg ripe tomatoes, roughly
   chopped
1 cucumber, peeled and
   roughly chopped
2 garlic cloves, peeled and
   crushed
1 green pepper, deseeded and
   roughly chopped
½ red onion, peeled and
   roughly chopped
125ml olive oil
1–2 tbsp sherry vinegar
½ tsp ground cumin
sea salt and black pepper

This spicy cold tomato soup is one of my favourite summer recipes. It's easy to make, healthy and fresh tasting, and a fantastic choice on a hot summer day. But although this is a super summer recipe, don't hesitate to prepare it all year round – friends and family will love it. In the last few years, **Godello** has become one of the most exciting Spanish white varieties. This grape offers a range of styles, any of which will match well with gazpacho.

1. Put all the vegetables in a blender. Start to blend, adding the olive oil in a gentle stream as you do so. Keep blending until you have a soup with a really smooth texture. Once smooth add the vinegar and cumin, and season with salt and black pepper. Taste and adjust the seasoning as necessary.

2. Pour the gazpacho into a container with a lid. Cover and put in the fridge for at least 30 minutes to chill well and allow all the flavours to mingle.

3. Serve with a swirl of olive oil

# GRÜNER VELTLINER

**HOME COUNTRY: AUSTRIA**

——

**OTHER COUNTRIES:
CZECH REPUBLIC, SLOVAKIA**

——

**MAIN REGIONS: KAMPTAL,
KREMSTAL, WACHAU**

——

**FAMOUS APPELLATIONS:
KAMPTAL, KREMSTAL,
WACHAU**

——

**SWEETNESS: DRY**

——

**FRUITS: HIGH**

——

**ACIDITY: HIGH**

——

**ALCOHOL: MEDIUM**

——

**BODY: MEDIUM**

——

**GLASSWARE: WHITE**

——

**TEMPERATURE:
WELL CHILLED**

——

**CELLAR: 3 YEARS**

——

**BUDGET: ££**

Grüner Veltliner is a white grape that hails from Austria. Depending on the terroir, this grape can produce soft wines that possess strong mineral notes. Grapes from the steep slopes of the best vineyards can yield an age-worthy wine, giving riper flavours with white pepper, citrus and even celery. With time in bottle, these wines age gracefully becoming nutty and developing a honeyed note, while maintaining their zip.

**STYLES:**
Unoaked Grüner Veltliner is predominantly characterised by citrus fruits, white pepper and celery. When bottle aged, the wine gains richness, with nutty and honeyed complexity.

**FLAVOURS:**
Lemon, lime, apple, white peach, celery, white pepper, nuts

# VEGGIE COUSCOUS

**SERVES: 4**

---

**TIME: 30 MINS**

---

**VEGETARIAN**

---

1 red pepper, deseeded and chopped into bite-sized pieces

1 yellow pepper, deseeded and chopped into bite-sized pieces

1 sweet potato, peeled and chopped into bite-sized pieces

1 courgette, thickly sliced

1 red onion, cut into thin wedges

3 tbsp olive oil

1 tsp dried chilli flakes

250g couscous

300ml hot vegetable stock

200g cooked beetroot, cut into small dice

250g cherry tomatoes, halved

25g mint leaves, roughly chopped

200g feta, crumbled

zest and juice of 1 lemon

sea salt and black pepper

This is a versatile dish that works as both a main course or as a side dish, and it reheats well if you have some leftovers. The combination of the roasted flavour of the vegetables with the texture of the couscous is delicious. **Grüner Veltliner** has zingy acidity and savoury notes that will match perfectly with this couscous.

1. Preheat the oven to 200°C/gas 6.

2. Put the peppers, sweet potato, courgette and onion on to a large baking tray. Add the olive oil, dried chilli and season with salt and pepper. Mix well so all the vegetables are coated in the oil and roast for 25 minutes, or until tender and golden.

3. While the vegetables are roasting, put the couscous into a large bowl. Add the hot stock, then cover and set aside for around 10 minutes until all the liquid has been absorbed.

4. Fluff the cooked couscous with a fork to separate the grains, then add the roasted vegetables, along with the beetroot and tomatoes and toss well. Add the mint and crumbled feta to the bowl along with the lemon zest and juice. Toss once more and check the seasoning before serving.

# MARSANNE / ROUSSANNE

**HOME COUNTRY: FRANCE**
—

**OTHER COUNTRIES:**
**AUSTRALIA, AUSTRIA, NEW**
**ZEALAND, SWITZERLAND**
—

**MAIN REGIONS:**
**LANGUEDOC-ROUSSILLON,**
**RHÔNE VALLEY**
—

**FAMOUS APPELLATIONS:**
**CHÂTEAUNEUF-DU-PAPE,**
**CÔTES DU RHÔNE,**
**CROZES-HERMITAGE,**
**HERMITAGE, SAINT-JOSEPH**
—

**SWEETNESS: DRY**
—

**FRUITS: MEDIUM**
—

**ACIDITY: MEDIUM**
—

**ALCOHOL: MEDIUM TO HIGH**
—

**BODY: MEDIUM**
—

**GLASSWARE: WHITE**
—

**TEMPERATURE:**
**WELL CHILLED**
—

**CELLAR: 3–5 YEARS**
—

**BUDGET: ££–£££**

The Rhône Valley in France is home to the aromatic Marsanne and Roussanne grapes. Of the two, Marsanne is easiest to grow and needs to be kept from over producing. Roussanne is a much more challenging grape to grow. Each can stand alone as a varietal wine, but they really shine when blended together. Marsanne lends texture and flavours of orange and apricot while the more elegant Roussanne contributes herbal notes and wonderful minerality. Roussanne and Marsanne are the only white varieties permitted in the blend for the famous appellations of Crozes-Hermitage, Hermitage and St-Joseph.

**STYLES:**
Marsanne-based blends can produce wines with some body and lovely flavours of orange and apricot. They can be deeply coloured wines that, with age, develop a honeyed and nutty component with a waxy texture. Roussanne-based blends are dominated by aromatic notes, like herbal tea and pears, gaining floral and nutty nuances as the wine ages. It's interesting to note that Roussanne is low in acidity and yet has remarkable ability to age.

**FLAVOURS:**
Lemon, lime, orange, pear, peach, apricot, white pepper, jasmine, honey, herbs and mineral notes

# GREEK SALMON

**SERVES: 4**

—

**TIME: 35 MINS**

—

1½ red onions: 1 sliced,
　½ finely chopped
2 lemons: 1 thinly sliced,
　1 juiced
4 salmon fillets
olive oil, for drizzling
250g cherry tomatoes, halved
1 cucumber, cut into large dice
50g Kalamata olives, pitted
　and torn
200g feta, cut into dice

FOR THE DRESSING
3 tbsp extra virgin olive oil
1 garlic clove, crushed
2 tbsp chopped fresh dill,
　plus extra to serve
1 tbsp chopped fresh oregano
sea salt and black pepper

I adore Greek cuisine because their dishes exemplify the best of the Mediterranean diet. I've visited their beautiful country many times over the years, and I am always impressed with how well they combine simple, fresh, healthy ingredients to make great tasting dishes. A good salmon fillet accompanied by fresh vegetables and feta is a guaranteed winner. An elegant white Rhône blend of **Marsanne** and **Roussanne** will work well as an accompaniment, thanks to its soft texture and lush fruits.

1. Preheat the oven to 180ºC/gas 4.

2. Put the sliced red onion and lemon at the bottom of a baking tray large enough to accommodate all the salmon fillets. Place the fillets on top, skin side up. Give everything a splash of olive oil and season with salt and black pepper. Bake for 15–20 minutes until the fish is cooked through and the lemon and onion slices have softened.

3. Put the tomatoes, cucumber, olives, chopped red onion and feta in a large bowl.

4. In a jar or jug, combine all the dressing ingredients and mix well.

5. Drizzle the salad with the dressing and toss everything together. Serve with the salmon and roasted lemon and onion, scattering over more dill to finish.

# PECORINO

**HOME COUNTRY: ITALY**

**MAIN REGIONS:**
**ABRUZZO, MARCHE**

**FAMOUS APPELLATIONS:**
**COLLI MACERATESI,**
**FALERIO DEI COLLI**
**ASCOLANI, OFFIDA**

**SWEETNESS: DRY**

**FRUITS: MEDIUM**

**ACIDITY: HIGH**

**ALCOHOL: MEDIUM**

**BODY: MEDIUM**

**GLASSWARE: WHITE**

**TEMPERATURE: CHILLED**

**CELLAR: 1–2 YEARS**

**BUDGET: £**

Pecorino is an old white grape variety that is currently enjoying renewed interest. The name is derived from the Italian word 'pecora' meaning 'sheep' (Pecorino is also the name of the local sheeps' cheese). The grape originally comes from Marche, on Italy's east coast, where local lore says that it earned its name because it was the favourite snack of sheep. Pecorino is an aromatic, adaptable grape with high acidity that is commonly found as a varietal, or as a dominant or supporting variety in a blend.

**STYLES:**
Generally found in a light style, the wine shows a floral character with accents of citrus and stone fruits. When more complex, wines are richer in style with tropical fruits, hints of honey and nuttiness.

**FLAVOURS:**
Lemon, lime, pear, peach, ginger, acacia, nuts

# PARMIGIANA DI MELANZANE
## [BAKED AUBERGINE WITH TOMATO & PARMESAN]

**SERVES: 4**

---

**TIME: 60 MINS**

---

**VEGETARIAN**

---

4 large aubergines, sliced
   lengthways 5mm thick
1 tbsp olive oil, plus extra
   for brushing
2 garlic cloves, crushed
3 x 400g tins chopped
   tomatoes
a bunch of basil leaves,
   chopped
3 eggs, hard-boiled, peeled
   and sliced
200g Parmesan, grated
1 ball of mozzarella, torn
sea salt and black pepper

As you peruse this book, it will become clear that I am in love with aubergine. It's a great ingredient due to its firm texture and appealing flavour, and is an amazing option when you are looking to make a vegetarian dish. This parmigiana is intended to be served hot, but the leftovers are fantastic cold. The high acidity and aromatic fruits of **Pecorino** will complement the flavourful *parmigiana di melanzane*.

1. Preheat the oven to 180°C/gas 4 and line 2 large baking trays with baking paper.

2. Lay the aubergine slices side by side on the prepared baking tray, making sure they are not overlapping. Brush each slice with olive oil and season with salt and pepper on both sides. Bake for 25–30 minutes until tender, turning halfway through.

3. Meanwhile, heat the tablespoon of olive oil in a saucepan over a medium heat, add the garlic and cook for just 1 minute until golden. Add the tinned tomatoes, bring to a simmer and cook gently for 20 minutes until slightly reduced. Season with salt and pepper and add the basil.

4. Once the aubergines are ready, get a large baking dish and put some tomato sauce at the bottom. Add a layer of aubergine, then one of eggs, followed by a sprinkling of Parmesan and then more tomato sauce. Repeat until you have used all the aubergines. Top up the last layer of aubergines with the mozzarella and more Parmesan. Bake for 20–30 minutes until golden.

# PICPOUL

**HOME COUNTRY: FRANCE**

**OTHER COUNTRIES: SPAIN**

**MAIN REGIONS: CATALUNYA, LANGUEDOC-ROUSSILLON, RHÔNE VALLEY**

**FAMOUS APPELLATIONS: LANGUEDOC, PICPOUL DE PINET**

**SWEETNESS: DRY**

**FRUITS: HIGH**

**ACIDITY: HIGH**

**ALCOHOL: MEDIUM**

**BODY: FULL**

**GLASSWARE: WHITE**

**TEMPERATURE: CHILLED**

**CELLAR: 1–2 YEARS**

**BUDGET: £**

Picpoul, literally meaning 'lip stinger', earned its name thanks to its very high natural acidity – an important asset when growing in hot southern France. Picpoul has garnered a lot of attention recently, despite the fact that it's an old variety whose origins can be traced back to the 17th century. The best grapes are produced in the appellation of Picpoul de Pinet, where their zingy lemon flavour and high acidity make a refreshing wine.

**STYLES:**
Picpoul is most frequently found as a light wine with a lemony fruit character. It can also display other citrus and stone fruit aromas. It is a popular choice for blending in the Languedoc and Rhône Valley, where it makes more complex, rich wines with higher alcohol.

**FLAVOURS:**
Lemon, lime, orange, pear, apricot, white pepper, herbs

# SEABASS & QUINOA SALAD

**SERVES: 2**

—

**TIME: 20 MINS**

—

100g quinoa
4 tbsp extra virgin olive oil
juice of 1 lemon
½ tbsp sherry vinegar
60g rocket
1 avocado, peeled, pitted and
    cut into chunks
200g cherry tomatoes, halved
2 seabass fillets
sea salt and black pepper

For centuries, quinoa has been an important dietary staple of the people of South America. Nutritious and rich in protein and fibre, quinoa is still a favoured grain in Chile. Seabass is also a classic feature on Chilean menus, and pairing quinoa with seabass makes for a wonderful, quick meal. The **Picpoul** grape, with its zesty personality, is a perfect match for just about any fish or seafood dish, including this one.

1.  Rinse the quinoa well under cold water and put it into a saucepan. Cover with water and bring to the boil, then reduce the heat and simmer, covered, for 15 minutes until the grains are tender. Drain and place in a bowl to cool.

2.  For the dressing, blend 3 tablespoons of the oil with the lemon juice, vinegar, and some salt and black pepper and set aside.

3.  Once the quinoa has cooled, add the rocket, avocado and tomatoes, then add the dressing and mix well.

4.  Heat the remaining 1 tablespoon olive oil in a frying pan over a medium heat. Season the seabass fillets, then place them in the pan, skin side down. Cook for 3 minutes until the skin is crisp and golden, then turn over and cook for another 1 minute to cook the fish through. Remove from the pan and serve with the quinoa salad.

# PINOT GRIS [PINOT GRIGIO]

**HOME COUNTRY: FRANCE**
—

**OTHER COUNTRIES:
AUSTRALIA, GERMANY,
ITALY, NEW ZEALAND, USA**
—

**MAIN REGIONS: ALSACE,
FRIULI, PFALZ, TRENTINO-
ALTO ADIGE, VENETO**
—

**FAMOUS APPELLATIONS:
ALSACE, FRIULI, PFALZ,
TRENTINO-ALTO ADIGE,
VENETO**
—

**SWEETNESS: DRY TO SWEET**
—

**FRUITS: HIGH**
—

**ACIDITY: MEDIUM**
—

**ALCOHOL: MEDIUM TO HIGH**
—

**BODY: MEDIUM TO FULL**
—

**GLASSWARE: WHITE**
—

**TEMPERATURE:
WELL CHILLED**
—

**CELLAR: 1–2 YEARS**
—

**BUDGET: £–££**

Pinot Gris, thought to be a mutation of Pinot Noir, originated in Burgundy in France. The best examples of this grape now come from Alsace. This region has an ideal climate for growing grapes – here, the fruit is able to fully ripen and the subsequent wines display an amazing honeyed personality with lush fruits and spicy accents. The exact style varies depending upon location and yields. This grape has delicious fruit character, intense aromas, soft texture and great minerality. Some producers use skin contact to improve the intensity and complexity of the final wine. This is a winemaking technique that is very common when the producer wishes to create a richer white wine.

**STYLES:**
Light examples are found in Friuli in northern Italy. These wines are aromatic and full of citrus and stone fruits. More complex styles come from Alsace (France), Pfalz and Baden (Germany), where the wines have tropical fruit flavours, such as melon, spice and honey. Sweet wines from Alsace are full-bodied with even more pronounced honey and rich tropical fruit flavours.

**FLAVOURS:**
Lime, pear, apple, melon, peach, pineapple, almond, honey, spice

# SPICY AUBERGINE, FETA & POMEGRANATE

**SERVES: 4**

——

**TIME: 45 MINS**

——

**VEGETARIAN**

——

4 large aubergines, sliced
 lengthways into 5mm thick
 slices
4 tbsp olive oil
1 tsp chilli flakes
200g feta, crumbled
a bunch of parsley, roughly
 chopped
a bunch of mint leaves,
 roughly chopped
1 pomegranate, seeds only
zest and juice of 1 lemon
sea salt and black pepper

If you like contrasts of texture and flavour, this recipe is for you. Aubergine is a 'meaty' vegetable, with great density and texture. Feta adds acidity, saltiness and a creamy texture. Rounding out this attractive dish is pomegranate which contributes a touch of sweetness. With a full-bodied **Pinot Gris**, the ripe stone fruits and a honeyed character will create a pleasing balance between food and wine.

1. Heat a griddle pan over a high heat and, working in batches, griddle the aubergine slices until soft through and nicely charred on both sides. Once cooked, drizzle with the olive oil and season with salt, black pepper and chilli flakes, making sure each slice is nicely coated.

2. Arrange the aubergine slices on a large serving platter and top with the feta, parsley, mint and pomegranate seeds. Sprinkle over the lemon zest and squeeze over the juice, and serve.

# RIESLING

**HOME COUNTRY: GERMANY**

**OTHER COUNTRIES: AUSTRALIA, AUSTRIA, FRANCE, NEW ZEALAND, USA**

**MAIN REGIONS: ALSACE, CLARE VALLEY, EDEN VALLEY, MOSEL, PFALZ, RHEINGAU**

**FAMOUS APPELLATIONS: ALSACE, MOSEL, PFALZ, RHEINGAU**

**SWEETNESS: DRY TO SWEET**

**FRUITS: HIGH**

**ACIDITY: HIGH**

**ALCOHOL: LOW TO MEDIUM**

**BODY: LIGHT TO FULL**

**GLASSWARE: WHITE**

**TEMPERATURE: CHILLED**

**BUDGET: £-£££**

Riesling is one of the most exciting aromatic grape varieties – its versatility and ability to express terroir make it exceptional. Add high acidity and a huge range of fruit aromas and floral notes and you've got a real winner. Many of the best examples of Riesling have the ability to age well and, over time, develop even more complexity. An aroma commonly referred to as 'petrol' is unique to Riesling.

**STYLES:**
In the Mosel, Germany's coolest vineyard, a light-bodied floral wine is produced, with citrus fruits and green apple flavours. More complex styles come from warmer regions, especially Pfalz, where the wines are full of tropical fruits and honey, and have more body. In Germany, Auslese is a ripe style of white wine that can be dry or lightly sweet. Grapes affected by noble rot are used to make sweet styles of wine called Beerenauslese (sweet) and Trockenbeerenauslese (very sweet). Eiswein is another sweet style, which is made with ripe, non-botrytised grapes creating a wine with pure fruit flavours (see page 176 for more on sweet Riesling). Sparkling wines are also made with Riesling.

**FLAVOURS:**
Lemon, lime, apple, pear, pineapple, papaya, petrol, honey, floral notes

**CELLAR:**
Young wines should be consumed as soon as possible. Top wines can age for 10–15+ years. The very best ones will age for decades.

# GRILLED TROUT, CUCUMBER & APPLE SALAD

**SERVES: 4**

——

**TIME: 30 MINS**

——

olive oil, for greasing and
   drizzling
4 small whole trout,
   cleaned and gutted
2 garlic cloves, crushed
a small bunch of dill
1 lemon, thinly sliced, plus
   extra wedges to serve
sea salt and black pepper

FOR THE SALAD:
160g watercress
2 cucumbers, julienned
   (leave the skin on)
2 apples, julienned
3 tbsp olive oil
juice of 1 lemon
2 tsp honey
1 tsp Dijon mustard

I think that trout is too often ignored when it comes to selecting fish for a recipe. Trout is delicate, has great texture and can be good value. In this recipe, the goal is to allow the flavours of the fish to shine by not adding anything too strong to the mix. A perfect complement is this fresh salad of cucumber and watercress that incorporates a surprise: apple! The high acidity and aromatic character of **Riesling** makes a fabulous partner for this tantalising dish.

1. Preheat the oven to 220°C/gas 7 and lightly oil a baking tray.

2. Lay the trout on the prepared baking tray. Season the inside of each trout with salt and pepper, add the crushed garlic and drizzle in some olive oil. Equally distribute the dill between the fish cavities.

3. Make two diagonal cuts on the outside of each fish and stuff the slits with a slice of lemon, putting the rest of the slices inside the fish cavities. Season the outside of the fish with salt and pepper and drizzle some more olive oil. Place in the oven and bake for 15–20 minutes until cooked through.

4. While the trout is cooking, put the watercress, cucumbers and apples in a large bowl.

5. Whisk together the olive oil, half the lemon juice, honey and Dijon mustard. Season to taste and dress the salad.

6. Once the fish is cooked, squeeze some lemon juice over before serving with the salad.

'Riesling is one of the most exciting aromatic grape varieties – its versatility and ability to express terroir make it exceptional'

RIESLING WITH GRILLED TROUT, CUCUMBER & APPLE SALAD

# SAUVIGNON BLANC

**HOME COUNTRY: FRANCE**

**OTHER COUNTRIES: CHILE, NEW ZEALAND, SOUTH AFRICA, USA**

**MAIN REGIONS: BORDEAUX, CASABLANCA, ELGIN, LOIRE, MARLBOROUGH, NAPA VALLEY**

**FAMOUS APPELLATIONS: BORDEAUX, POUILLY-FUMÉ, SANCERRE**

**SWEETNESS: DRY TO SWEET**

**FRUITS: HIGH**

**ACIDITY: HIGH**

**ALCOHOL: MEDIUM**

**BODY: LIGHT TO FULL**

**GLASSWARE: WHITE**

**TEMPERATURE: WELL CHILLED**

**CELLAR: 2–3 YEARS FOR YOUNG WINES. TOP WINES 15+ YEARS. SAUTERNES CAN AGE FOR DECADES.**

**BUDGET: £–£££**

Sauvignon Blanc is an aromatic grape variety that can produce markedly different wines in different locations. No matter the climate, the grape always maintains its very high acidity. In cooler climates, wines tend to be light bodied with citrus and vegetal aromas such as grass. In warmer areas the wine shows more intense fruit flavours, leaning towards peach, apricot and passion fruit.

**STYLES:**
In the Loire, in France, the 'European home' of Sauvignon Blanc, the wines are unoaked. This makes for a refreshing, aromatic wine with predominantly green and citrus fruit flavours complemented by vegetal aromas. In Marlborough, on New Zealand's South Island, the 'New World home' of the grape, the wines are also unoaked and have very distinctive gooseberry and passion fruit flavours. Richer oaked styles come from Bordeaux, where Sauvignon Blanc is frequently blended with Semillon. In Sauternes, in the southern part of Bordeaux, a luscious sweet wine is made from the same blend of grapes (see page 180). The grapes used must be affected by noble rot and produce a wine with great intensity and complexity. These wines have additional flavours of orange marmalade, honey and dried apricot.

**FLAVOURS:**
Lemon, lime, gooseberry, peach, apricot, green peppers, asparagus, passion fruit

# CEVICHE WITH AVOCADO & MANGO

**SERVES: 4**

—

**TIME: 20 MINS**

—

400g seabass fillets (or any firm white fish), cut into small bite-sized pieces

1 red onion, very finely sliced into rings

juice of 3 limes

juice of 1 lemon

1 avocado, peeled, pitted and diced

1 mango, peeled, pitted and diced

1 fresh chilli, finely chopped

a thumb-sized piece of ginger, finely chopped

1 garlic clove, crushed

½ bunch of coriander, finely chopped

½ bunch of chives, finely chopped

2 tbsp olive oil

sea salt and black pepper

tortilla chips, to serve

Ceviche (cured fish) is extremely popular along the Pacific coast of Latin America. I have suggested using seabass here, but any white fish can be used to make this dish. The addition of avocado, mango and a variety of herbs creates a great combination of flavours. Chile produces fantastic examples of **Sauvignon Blanc** that have excellent acidity with ripe stone fruits, perfect with this tasty ceviche.

1. Combine the fish and onion in a large glass bowl and squeeze over the juice of the limes and the lemon. Mix it well and let it rest for 5–10 minutes, or until the fish is just beginning to turn opaque.

2. After the marinating time, add all the remaining ingredients. Season with salt and pepper and serve immediately with tortilla chips for scooping.

'Chile produces fantastic examples of Sauvignon Blanc that have excellent acidity with ripe stone fruits, perfect with this tasty ceviche'

SAUVIGNON BLANC & CEVICHE WITH AVOCADO & MANGO

# SEMILLON

**HOME COUNTRY: FRANCE**

**OTHER COUNTRIES: AUSTRALIA, CHILE, SOUTH AFRICA**

**MAIN REGIONS: BORDEAUX, FRANSCHHOEK, HUNTER VALLEY, MAIPO VALLEY**

**FAMOUS APPELLATIONS: BARSAC, ENTRE-DEUX-MERS, GRAVES, PESSAC-LÉOGNAN, SAUTERNES**

**SWEETNESS: DRY TO SWEET**

**FRUITS: MEDIUM**

**ACIDITY: LOW TO MEDIUM**

**ALCOHOL: MEDIUM**

**BODY: MEDIUM TO FULL**

**GLASSWARE: WHITE**

**TEMPERATURE: WELL CHILLED**

**CELLAR: 2–3 YEARS FOR YOUNG WINES. TOP WINES 15+ YEARS. SAUTERNES CAN AGE FOR DECADES.**

**BUDGET: £–£££**

Semillon can be grown in most wine regions, albeit not completely successfully. When the grapes are handled properly and grown in suitable locations, the wines can be vibrant and interesting. Southwest France is Semillon's natural home and in Bordeaux young wines from humble vineyards are delicious within 3–5 years of bottling. Better vineyards can make wines that have longevity and complexity. In the 'Bordeaux blend' Semillon is blended with Sauvignon Blanc to make both dry and sweet wines. The Hunter Valley in Australia is also making some exciting wines, especially when grapes are harvested at the optimum time to balance the fruit and alcohol content while retaining good levels of acidity.

**STYLES:**
Unoaked examples found in Bordeaux are refreshing wines with good acidity thanks to the addition of Sauvignon Blanc, which lends them elegance and finesse. Semillon grapes affected with noble rot and blended with Sauvignon Blanc produce sweet wines of amazing complexity. In the Hunter Valley, oaked versions use ripe grapes to make a wine filled with lush stone and tropical fruits and notes of vanilla from the oak. In Chile and South Africa notable examples are also produced with intense fruit character.

**FLAVOURS:**
Lemon, lime, apple, peach, pineapple, honey, nuts

# ISRAELI SALAD

**SERVES: 2**

—

**TIME: 15 MINS**

—

**VEGETARIAN**

—

1 cucumber, diced
250g cherry tomatoes,
    quartered
1 red onion, finely chopped
a bunch of parsley, finely
    chopped
2 tbsp olive oil
2 tbsp lemon juice
½ tsp sea salt
warm pita bread, to serve

FOR THE TZATZIKI:
1 cucumber
400g Greek yoghurt
1 garlic clove, crushed
juice of 1 lemon
a bunch of fresh mint, leaves
    finely chopped
1 tbsp extra virgin olive oil

In my travels I have learned that there is a lot of diversity when it comes to food culture, but also many similarities. This Israeli salad is an example of a typical Mediterranean dish and similar versions can be found all around the Mediterranean, especially in countries such as Turkey and Greece. Using only fresh ingredients, simply combined, it bursts with flavour. Serve it as a main course or a side dish. It pairs well with warm pita bread and fresh tzatziki. **Semillon** wines have great fruit character and an interesting texture that will nicely complement this enjoyable dish.

1. Mix together all the vegetables and herbs in a serving bowl. Dress with the olive oil, lemon juice and salt, and toss well to combine.

2. To make the tzatziki, grate the cucumber, then use your hands to squeeze out any excess water.

3. Combine the cucumber, yoghurt, garlic, lemon juice and a good handful of the chopped fresh mint leaves. Add the olive oil and season with salt and black pepper to taste.

4. Serve the salad with warm pita bread and the tzatziki.

# TORRONTÉS

**HOME COUNTRY:**
**ARGENTINA**

—

**OTHER COUNTRIES:**
**CHILE, URUGUAY**

—

**MAIN REGIONS:**
**MENDOZA, SALTA**

—

**SWEETNESS: DRY AND**
**OFF-DRY**

—

**FRUITS: HIGH**

—

**ACIDITY: MEDIUM**

—

**ALCOHOL: MEDIUM**

—

**BODY: MEDIUM**

—

**GLASSWARE: WHITE**

—

**TEMPERATURE: CHILLED**

—

**CELLAR: 2 YEARS**

—

**BUDGET: £**

This grape is the most important white grape in Argentina. Torrontés best expresses its character when grown in the region of Salta, high in the Andes. In fact, there is a Torrontés vineyard planted at nearly 3,000 metres above sea level, which has the distinction of being the highest vineyard in the world. Vines grown at high altitudes benefit from cooler daily temperatures while still receiving plenty of sun to ripen the fruit. Nighttime is even cooler, giving the vines a chance to rest and allowing the grapes to maintain their natural high acidity. This makes for a delicious, refreshing wine. The aromas can be likened to that of Gewurtztraminer, but with less intensity.

**STYLES:**
Typically, Torrontés produces a light wine that is easy to drink, with floral, lightly spiced aromas and fruit flavours ranging from citrus to stone fruits. In general, these wines should be opened within no more than a couple of years of bottling as they do not age well.

**FLAVOURS:**
Lemon, lime, lychee, rose petals, melon, honey, peach, apricot

# STIR-FRIED RICE WITH PRAWNS

**SERVES: 2**

———

**TIME: 20 MINS**

———

2 tbsp sunflower oil
1 garlic clove, crushed
1 red chilli, finely diced
200g raw king prawns, peeled
200g frozen peas
250g cooked and cooled
   Thai jasmine rice (ideally
   from the previous day)
1–2 tbsp soy sauce
zest and juice of 1 lime
black pepper

Sometimes it's difficult to summon enough energy to cook something nice after a long day of work. Stir-fried rice with prawns is a great option as it works best with day-old rice and so you can use up leftovers, too. Since the rice is already cooked, and prawns are quick to cook – as well as being delicious and nutritious – this dish can be on the table in no time. All that needs to be added are some seasonings and vegetables. My recipe includes peas, but you can incorporate just about any vegetable that you've got in your kitchen. **Torrontés** is an aromatic grape variety that offers incredible stone fruit flavours. The complexity of the wine will pair well with this spicy dish.

1. Heat 1 tablespoon of the sunflower oil in a frying pan or wok over a medium heat. Add the garlic and red chilli and stir fry for 1 minute, then add the prawns and cook for a further 3 minutes, stirring constantly.

2. Add the peas and cook for another 3 minutes.

3. Add the remaining oil and the rice to the pan. Stir-fry everything together for another several minutes, allowing the rice to brown and making sure it is completely heated through. Season with soy sauce, to taste, and black pepper.

4. Add the lime zest and juice, to serve.

# VERDEJO

**HOME COUNTRY: SPAIN**

**MAIN REGIONS: CASTILLA Y LEÓN**

**FAMOUS APPELLATIONS: CIGALES, RUEDA, TORO**

**SWEETNESS: DRY**

**FRUITS: MEDIUM TO HIGH**

**ACIDITY: MEDIUM**

**ALCOHOL: MEDIUM**

**BODY: FULL**

**GLASSWARE: WHITE**

**TEMPERATURE: WELL CHILLED**

**CELLAR: 3 YEARS**

**BUDGET: £**

The origin of the Verdejo grape is unknown, although many believe that it originated in Rueda, Spain. The name Verdejo is a take on the Spanish word 'verde' meaning green, since the ripe grapes are a bright green colour. The vineyards of Verdejo were nearly decimated by phylloxera, but have been making a comeback since the 1970s. In Rueda, the best region for highlighting the qualities of this grape, wines with loads of flavour, structure and exhilarating acidity can be produced. Verdejo has a tendency to oxidise easily, so care needs to be taken during harvest and vinification.

**STYLES:**

It is common to find varietal wines that are unoaked. These wines are pale lemon with zesty flavours of fennel and citrus and herbal notes similar to Sauvignon Blanc. They are best drunk young, but some will gain a honeyed and nutty complexity with a few years of bottle ageing. Some producers are making more complex wines with either skin contact and/or some barrel fermentation or ageing. This adds more complexity, but the wood must be used judiciously so as not to overpower the varietal character of the wine. Blended wines are also very common. By law there must be no less than 50 per cent Verdejo blended with a combination of Viura and/or Sauvignon Blanc.

**FLAVOURS:**

Lemon, lime, apple, pear, melon, nuts, honey, floral notes

# PADRÓN PEPPERS

**SERVES: 4**

——

**TIME: 5 MINS**

——

**VEGETARIAN**

——

1 tbsp olive oil
500g padrón peppers,
  washed and dried
sea salt

This vegetarian snack is quick and easy and has a bit of a kick. **Verdejo** is an amazing grape that is making a spectacular comeback in the wine world. Its great structure and pure fruit flavours are responsible for its steadily increasing popularity.

1. Heat the oil in a large frying pan over a high heat. Add the peppers and fry, stirring frequently, for about 5 minutes until the peppers are soft and charred.

2. Place the peppers on a plate or a board. Season with plenty of sea salt and serve.

'In Rueda, Verdejo wines with loads of flavour, structure and exhilarating acidity can be produced'

VERDEJO WITH PADRÓN PEPPERS

# VERDELHO

**HOME COUNTRY: PORTUGAL**

**OTHER COUNTRIES: AUSTRALIA, NEW ZEALAND, SPAIN**

**MAIN REGIONS: GALICIA, HUNTER VALLEY, MADEIRA**

**FAMOUS APPELLATIONS: MADEIRA VERDELHO, VINHO DO DÃO**

**SWEETNESS: DRY TO SWEET**

**FRUITS: HIGH**

**ACIDITY: MEDIUM TO HIGH**

**ALCOHOL: MEDIUM TO HIGH**

**BODY: FULL**

**GLASSWARE: WHITE**

**TEMPERATURE: CHILLED**

**CELLAR: 2 YEARS FOR YOUNG DRY WINES. FORTIFIED WINES CAN AGE FOR DECADES.**

**BUDGET: £–£££**

Verdelho is another very old variety dating back to 15th-century Portugal, and specifically the island of Madeira. Originally known for being one of the noble grapes used to produce a style of Madeira, the island's famous fortified wine, it is now also being used to produce some delicious dry wines. This grape should not be confused with Spain's white grape Verdejo (see page 86). Verdelho is an aromatic grape that has extremely high acidity with a mix of citrus, stone fruits and floral notes. The Spanish region of Galicia produces exciting examples of Verdelho. Australia is producing small quantities of high-quality dry Verdelho wines that display ripe lemon flavours and sweet honeysuckle.

**STYLES:**
Verdelho was originally used to make the fortified wine Madeira – a complex wine with very ripe fruits and a high alcohol content. The newer trend is to produce dry wines with bracing acidity and flavours ranging from citrus to stone fruits. When the grapes are allowed to ripen fully, lovely aromas of honeysuckle enhance the wine's profile.

**FLAVOURS:**
Lemon, lime, pear, apricot, spices, leaf and floral notes

# MUSSEL SOUP

**SERVES: 2**

—

**TIME: 30 MINS**

—

1kg mussels in shells
3 tbsp olive oil
1 white onion, finely sliced
1 carrot, peeled and finely
   diced
1 red pepper, julienned
2 garlic cloves, sliced
a pinch of dried chilli flakes
a pinch of ground cumin
a pinch of dried oregano
100g long grain rice
2 bay leaves
100ml whole milk
1 egg yolk
sea salt and black pepper

When I was growing up, my aunt Golla influenced me immensely in the kitchen. She taught me that it's vital to know how to cook, but it's even more important to have a connection to the ingredients you're cooking. My family enjoyed this mussel soup at nearly every Sunday lunch, and it's one I love to serve with a nice bottle of **Verdelho**.

1. Wash the mussels well, removing the beards and any barnacles. If any are open, give them a sharp tap – if they remain open, discard.

2. Heat a large saucepan over a medium heat and add the mussels. Cover them with 250ml water and bring to the boil. Turn down to a lively simmer, put the lid on, and cook for about 4 minutes, or until the shells have opened. Remove the mussels and set aside, reserving the broth the mussels were cooked in. Discard any mussels that haven't opened.

3. Heat the olive oil in another saucepan over a medium heat. Add the onion, carrot, red pepper and garlic. Cook gently until the onion is translucent and the vegetables have softened, about 10–15 minutes.

4. While the vegetables are cooking, remove most of the mussels from the shells, reserving a few in the shell for garnish.

5. Add the chilli flakes, cumin and oregano to the cooked vegetables and season with salt and black pepper. Stir to combine, then add the reserved broth, the rice and the bay leaves. Bring to the boil, turn the heat down and simmer for 8–10 minutes until the rice is cooked.

6. Add the milk and egg yolk and stir to incorporate, then add the deshelled mussels and heat through for another 2–3 minutes. Serve with a few mussels in shells on the top of each bowl.

# VERMENTINO

**HOME COUNTRY: ITALY**

**OTHER COUNTRIES: AUSTRALIA, FRANCE**

**MAIN REGIONS: CORSICA, LANGUEDOC-ROUSSILLON, LIGURIA, SARDINIA, TUSCANY**

**FAMOUS APPELLATIONS: BELLET, COLLI DI LUNI, PATRIMONIO, VERMENTINO DI GALLURA, VERMENTINO DI SARDEGNA**

**SWEETNESS: DRY**

**FRUITS: MEDIUM**

**ACIDITY: MEDIUM TO HIGH**

**ALCOHOL: MEDIUM**

**BODY: MEDIUM**

**GLASSWARE: WHITE**

**TEMPERATURE: WELL CHILLED**

**CELLAR: 1–2 YEARS**

**BUDGET: £**

Vermentino may be a Mediterranean grape variety, but its exact origin is hotly contested. Some say that it originated in Spain and was brought to Italy, while others have exactly the opposing view. The grape is found all over Italy although many of the best wines are made in Tuscany and Liguria (where it goes by the name Pigato). The island of Sardinia also produces some stellar examples. Good examples are also found in the south of France in Languedoc-Roussillon, where the grape is called Rolle. The grape does a good job of adapting to different climates and is typically Italian with its racy acidity. Vermentino displays pleasing aromas of green apple, lemon, peach and dried herbs, with some salinity on the palate.

**STYLES:**
When unoaked and youthful these wines are a delight to drink, with their crisp style, salinity and abundance of fruits. Don't wait – there's nothing to be gained from letting them age in the bottle.

**FLAVOURS:**
Lemon, lime, apple, pear, pineapple, herbs, salty notes

# PANZANELLA
## [BREAD SALAD]

**SERVES: 4**

——

**TIME: 20 MINS**

——

**VEGETARIAN**

——

5 tbsp olive oil

2 garlic cloves, crushed

1 tsp dried chilli flakes

150g ciabatta bread, torn in 2–3cm chunks

600g ripe tomatoes (use a mix of colours), chopped in 4cm chunks

1 ripe avocado, peeled, pitted and chopped

1 tbsp capers, roughly chopped

a handful of parsley, leaves picked

a handful of basil, leaves picked

zest and juice of 1 lemon

Panzanella has its humble beginnings in Italy on the 'Mare Nostrum', as the ancient Romans called the Mediterranean. It was traditionally made at home, with day-old bread that was soaked in water, as it's a brilliant way to revive slightly stale bread. Whether you have some day-old bread around or chose to use fresh, you won't go wrong with this salad. **Vermentino** is a Mediterranean grape, with a crisp acidity and mix of aromas that will be a real pleaser with the panzanella.

1. Heat the olive oil in a frying pan over a low heat. Add the garlic and chilli and cook for 1–2 minutes until the garlic is beginning to turn golden. Add the bread and a good pinch of sea salt and toss gently, making sure that all the pieces get coated in the chilli and garlic oil. Cook for another few minutes, stirring gently, until the bread is golden and crunchy. Remove the bread to a plate lined with kitchen towel to drain and cool.

2. Put the tomatoes, avocado, capers, basil, parsley and lemon juice in a large serving bowl. Once cooled, add the bread to the bowl and toss the salad gently.

3. Before serving, sprinkle over the lemon zest.

'Vermentino displays pleasing aromas of green apple, lemon, peach and dried herbs'

VERMENTINO WITH PANZANELLA

# VIOGNIER

**HOME COUNTRY: FRANCE**
—

**OTHER COUNTRIES: AUSTRALIA, CHILE, NEW ZEALAND, USA**
—

**MAIN REGIONS: EDEN VALLEY, LANGUEDOC-ROUSSILLON, RHÔNE VALLEY**
—

**FAMOUS APPELLATIONS: CHÂTEAU GRILLET, CONDRIEU, CÔTE RÔTIE**
—

**SWEETNESS: DRY**
—

**FRUITS: HIGH**
—

**ACIDITY: LOW TO MEDIUM**
—

**ALCOHOL: MEDIUM TO HIGH**
—

**BODY: FULL**
—

**GLASSWARE: WHITE**
—

**TEMPERATURE: CHILLED**
—

**CELLAR: 2–3 YEARS**
—

**BUDGET: £–££**

Viognier can produce amazing, aromatic wines that are a joy to drink. However, this grape presents a challenge to grow as it has naturally low acidity and requires a substantial amount of sunlight and warmth to ripen adequately. Ripening the berries without lowering the acidity too much or producing an over-abundance of sugar (and therefore alcohol) requires skill and the right location. But with careful attention to detail in the vineyards and cellar, the winemaker can be rewarded with wines that have loads of body and texture, with ripe apricot and honey flavours.

**STYLES:**

It is said that the success of Viognier is made in the vineyard and not in the cellar. For the lightest examples there is minimal intervention in the cellar, which produces aromatic wines with stone fruits. With riper grapes comes richer tropical fruits and honey. In the quest for more complex wines, producers will use a few hours of skin contact and/or lees stirring to add body and a creamy texture. It is also not uncommon for producers to ferment in oak, although usually no more than 10–30 per cent new oak.

**FLAVOURS:**

Lemon, apple, peach, apricot, honey, herbs, floral notes

# COD, BROAD BEAN & PEA SALAD

**SERVES: 2**

———

**TIME: 20 MINS**

———

250g broad beans
   (frozen are fine)
200g peas (frozen are fine)
1 white onion, very finely
   chopped
a bunch of coriander,
   finely chopped
a bunch of chives, finely
   chopped
zest and juice of 1 lemon
4 tbsp olive oil, plus extra
   for drizzling
2 cod fillets
sea salt and black pepper

This is a classic recipe from my childhood in Chile. The flavours aren't complex, but with good, fresh ingredients it delivers a consistently delicious fish dish. As a bonus, it's quick to prepare, providing a healthy meal in a hurry. **Viognier** is always a great choice when serving fish. It's elegant with nice body and texture, and aromatic citrus and stone fruits.

1. Bring a pan of water to the boil, add the broad beans and peas and simmer together for 4 minutes – or 6 minutes if cooking from frozen. Drain and rinse with cold water, then place in a bowl to cool for a few minutes. If the outer skins of the broad beans are tough, you can remove them at this stage.

2. Mix the onion, coriander, chives, lemon juice and 2 tablespoons of the olive oil in a large glass bowl. Add the broad beans and peas to the bowl, season and mix well.

3. Heat the remaining 2 tablespoons of olive oil in a frying pan over a medium-high heat and place the cod fillets in, skin side down. Cook the cod for 3–4 minutes, until the skin is crisp and golden, then flip over and cook for another 1–2 minutes on the other side until the fish is cooked through and just opaque.

4. Divide the salad evenly between two plates and place a cod fillet on top. Sprinkle over the lemon zest and drizzle with a little more olive oil to serve.

# ROSÉ WINE

# ROSÉ

**HOME COUNTRIES:
FRANCE, ITALY, SPAIN**

**OTHER COUNTRIES:
THROUGHOUT THE
WINE WORLD**

**MAIN REGIONS: NAVARRA,
PROVENCE, VENETO**

**FAMOUS APPELLATIONS:
BARDOLINO CHIARETTO,
CÔTES DE PROVENCE,
NAVARRA, TAVEL**

**SWEETNESS: DRY AND
OFF-DRY**

**FRUITS: HIGH**

**ACIDITY: MEDIUM**

**ALCOHOL: MEDIUM**

**BODY: MEDIUM**

**GLASSWARE: WHITE**

**TEMPERATURE:
WELL CHILLED**

**CELLAR: 1 YEAR**

**BUDGET: £-££**

Rosé is believed to be the first type of wine to have been produced and drunk. The ancient Greeks and Romans were producing rosé using a mix of black and white grapes. The Greeks were also diluting their wine with water. It was a commonly held belief that only the uncultured drank undiluted wine! Today, to make rosé, black grapes are fermented with only minimal skin contact. The colour of red wines comes from the skin of the grapes, so just a little skin contact yields a pink or salmon coloured wine.

**STYLES:**
The styles of rosé can vary depending upon the varieties used and the hand of the winemaker. There are light, refreshing rosé wines that are very pale pink in colour. They are delicate with fresh fruit flavours. From here, rosé wines run the gamut all the way to those that are quite complex, salmon coloured and much richer in style.

**FLAVOURS:**
Orange, pear, strawberry, cherry, cranberry, redcurrant, floral notes

# GAMBAS AL AJILLO
## [GARLIC PRAWNS]

**SERVES: 2**

———

**TIME: 15 MINS**

———

2 tbsp olive oil
2 garlic cloves, finely sliced
½ tsp dried chilli flakes
250g large raw prawns,
    unpeeled
a good handful of parsley,
    finely chopped
juice of 1 lemon
sea salt and black pepper
warm crusty bread, to serve

I think about the ocean every time I make this dish. It's the perfect choice for aperitif time, preferably enjoyed while sat by the sea with a cool, crisp glass of wine. **Rosé** is a versatile wine that matches well with nearly every dish; try it with these prawns and you won't be disappointed!

1. Heat the olive oil in a large frying pan set over a medium heat. Add the garlic and chilli flakes and cook for about 1 minute, or until the garlic is golden.

2. Add the prawns, stir well and cook for around 5 minutes, until the prawns have turned pink and opaque and are cooked through.

3. Add the parsley and lemon juice. Stir well and season with salt and black pepper.

4. Serve the prawns with warm crusty bread to mop up the garlicky pan juices.

# RED WINE

# AGIORGITIKO

**HOME COUNTRY: GREECE**
—

**MAIN REGIONS: ATTICA, EPIRUS, MACEDONIA, NEMEA**
—

**FAMOUS APPELLATIONS: NEMEA**
—

**SWEETNESS: DRY**
—

**FRUITS: HIGH**
—

**ACIDITY: MEDIUM**
—

**ALCOHOL: MEDIUM**
—

**TANNINS: MEDIUM TO HIGH**
—

**BODY: MEDIUM TO HIGH**
—

**GLASSWARE: RED**
—

**TEMPERATURE: ROOM**
—

**CELLAR: 5-10 YEARS**
—

**BUDGET: £–££**

Agiorgitiko is one of the most important black grapes grown on the Peloponnese peninsula in southern Greece. This and Xinomavro, which dominates in the north of the country, are the most prized black grapes for winemaking. It grows best on the slopes of Nemea, at altitudes of between 250 and 800 metres, because Agiorgitiko requires the cooler temperatures that altitude provides to maintain its acidity. This variety can successfully be vinified in a wide variety of styles, ranging from light rosés and soft, fruity reds (made by carbonic maceration), to very bold, rich and spicy wines and sometimes even sweet wines with sun-dried grapes.

**STYLES:**
Light wines, produced from grapes grown at lower altitudes and frequently made using carbonic maceration, are easy drinking wines. The most complex wines come from the highest slopes, where the grapes can maintain their acidity. These spicy wines with big red fruit aromas are high in tannins and possess great ageing potential.

**FLAVOURS:**
Plum, blackberry, raspberry, pepper, toast

# MEATBALLS WITH TZATZIKI

**SERVES: 2**

——

**TIME: 30 MINS**

——

3 tbsp olive oil
1 onion, finely chopped
200g beef mince
a bunch of coriander,
   finely chopped
½ tsp dried thyme
1 tsp dried chilli flakes
sea salt and black pepper
Tzatziki (see page 41),
   to serve
pita bread, warmed,
   to serve

Street food has become so fashionable – perhaps because it reflects the authentic soul of a given region. I was inspired to cook this recipe after enjoying delicious lamb meatballs on the streets of Athens, although my recipe uses minced beef in place of lamb. With its spicy character, good acidity and mix of red and black fruits, **Agiorgitiko** is a lovely accompaniment.

1. Heat 1 tbsp of the oil in a small saucepan over a low–medium heat and gently cook the onion until soft and translucent, about 10 minutes. Set aside to cool.

2. Put the cooked onion, beef mince, coriander, thyme and chilli flakes in a large bowl. Season with salt and pepper. Use your hands to mix everything together until well combined, without over mixing. Divide the mix into 10 evenly sized portions and roll into balls.

3. Heat the remaining olive oil in a large frying pan over a medium heat. Add the meatballs and fry for around 6–8 minutes, turning them a couple of times during cooking. They are done when they are nicely browned on all sides and no longer pink in the middle.

4. Served the meatballs with fresh tzatziki and warm pita bread.

'Agiorgitiko is one of the most important black grapes grown on the Peloponnese peninsula in southern Greece'

AGIORGITIKO & MEATBALLS WITH TZATZIKI

# BARBERA

**HOME COUNTRY: ITALY**

**OTHER COUNTRIES: ARGENTINA, AUSTRALIA, USA**

**MAIN REGIONS: MENDOZA, NAPA VALLEY, PIEDMONT**

**FAMOUS APPELLATIONS: BARBERA D'ALBA, BARBERA D'ASTI, LANGHE, MONFERRATO, NIZZA**

**SWEETNESS: DRY**

**FRUITS: HIGH**

**ACIDITY: HIGH**

**ALCOHOL: MEDIUM**

**TANNINS: LOW**

**BODY: MEDIUM**

**GLASSWARE: RED**

**TEMPERATURE: ROOM**

**CELLAR: 3–5 YEARS**

**BUDGET: £–££**

As the third most-planted grape in Italy, Barbera is cultivated all over the country. Experts believe that the grape is indigenous to Piedmont in the northwest of Italy, where it can best display its assets. Barbera has high acidity, but unlike its big brother, Nebbiolo (see page 150), it is low in tannin and frequently lower in cost. Barbera is happiest when planted on warm sites. The wines range in style from youthful wines that are fresh and fruity to ones with more intensity, body and depth.

**STYLES:**
Fresh, youthful styles of Barbera display characteristic sour cherry flavours and are usually unoaked. Weightier versions are oaked and show rounder, softer fruits and spice from time in barrique.

**FLAVOURS:**
Cherry, strawberry, raspberry, plum, black pepper, toast, vanilla

# MOZZARELLA, TOMATOES, PEAS & BASIL

**SERVES: 2**

———

**TIME: 15 MINS**

———

**VEGETARIAN**

———

150g peas
2 balls of mozzarella
250g cherry tomatoes, halved
a bunch of basil, leaves picked
2 tbsp olive oil
zest of 1 lemon
sea salt and black pepper
ciabatta or focaccia bread,
   warmed, to serve

This is an extremely simple salad to prepare, which is fresh, tasty and beautiful with its mix of colours. It is a great option for a light lunch or a starter for the evening meal. What makes this recipe successful is the use of good quality, fresh ingredients. **Barbera** wines have refreshing acidity with lots of cherries and a bit of toast on the nose, which will be enhanced by this salad. Serve the wine slightly chilled or at room temperature.

1. In a small pan of boiling water, blanch the peas for a couple of minutes until tender, then run them under cold water in a colander and leave to drain.

2. Tear the mozzarella to into smaller pieces and scatter them over a large serving platter.

3. Distribute the tomatoes evenly among the cheese on the platter. Add the cooked peas and season with salt and pepper. Select the nicest basil leaves and add to the platter.

4. Drizzle the salad with the olive oil and sprinkle over the lemon zest.

5. Serve the salad with warm bread.

# CABERNET FRANC

**HOME COUNTRY: FRANCE**

**OTHER COUNTRIES: AUSTRALIA, CHILE, ITALY, USA**

**MAIN REGIONS: BORDEAUX, FRIULI, LOIRE VALLEY, NAPA VALLEY**

**FAMOUS APPELLATIONS: CHINON, POMEROL, SAINT EMILION**

**SWEETNESS: DRY**

**FRUITS: MEDIUM**

**ACIDITY: MEDIUM TO HIGH**

**ALCOHOL: MEDIUM**

**TANNINS: MEDIUM TO HIGH**

**BODY: MEDIUM TO HIGH**

**GLASSWARE: RED**

**TEMPERATURE: ROOM**

**CELLAR: 3–5 YEARS**

**BUDGET: £–£££**

Like so many grapes, the origin of Cabernet Franc is uncertain. It is possible that it is indigenous to its 'homeland' of Bordeaux in France, but it is equally likely that the grape originated in Spanish Basque Country and subsequently made its way to France. Unlike Cabernet Sauvignon (its offspring) it doesn't require as much heat and successfully ripens in years that are too cool for Cabernet Sauvignon. In a blend, it helps to balance acidity, add perfume and lovely fruit flavours and depth of colour. Elegant examples of Cabernet Franc varietals can be found in the New World.

**STYLES:**
The Loire Valley, with its cool soils such as clay and limestone, produces some great Cabernet Franc varietals that have a fresh style with a hint of wet stone minerality as well as raspberries and other red fruits and blackcurrant leaf. The most famous examples of Cabernet Franc in a blended wine come from Bordeaux, where the grape lends aroma, helps to lower acidity and adds spice and colour to the wine.

**FLAVOURS:**
Cherry, plum, blackberry, raspberry, blackcurrant leaf, black pepper, sweet spices, cigar, leather

# BEEF CARPACCIO

**SERVES: 4**

—

**TIME: 40 MINS**

—

a 400g piece of beef fillet
3–4 tbsp extra virgin olive oil
juice of 1 lemon
100g rocket
2 tsp capers, drained and
  rinsed
3 tbsp sun-dried tomatoes,
  roughly chopped
sea salt and black pepper
ciabatta or focaccia bread,
  to serve

The Italians usually eat carpaccio during the summer months when it is too hot to heat up the kitchen with a lot of cooking. Do as they do in Italy and try this on a warm summer's day. If you have a great butcher, it's best to get your meat there and have it finely sliced for you. It will be easier and save time. **Cabernet Franc** may seem an unusual match but with its amazing black fruits, intense aromas and a firm structure it works beautifully.

1. If the beef is not already sliced by your butcher, place it in the freezer until is half-frozen (about 15–20 minutes). Remove from the freezer and cut into very thin slices using a very sharp knife. Cover the slices with clingfilm and store in the fridge until you are ready to serve.

2. Make your dressing by whisking together the olive oil and lemon juice, and season with salt and black pepper.

3. Remove the carpaccio (beef) from the fridge and lay loosely on a large serving plate. Drizzle some of the dressing on top and season well.

4. Toss the rocket with the remaining dressing, and place in the centre of the plate. Scatter the capers and tomatoes evenly on top of the carpaccio.

5. Serve with ciabatta or focaccia.

'Cabernet Franc varietals from the Loire Valley have a fresh style, with a hint of wet stone minerality as well as raspberries and other red fruits and blackcurrant leaf'

CABERNET FRANC WITH BEEF CARPACCIO

# CABERNET SAUVIGNON

**HOME COUNTRY: FRANCE**

**OTHER COUNTRIES: AUSTRALIA, CHILE, ITALY, USA**

**MAIN REGIONS: BORDEAUX, MAIPO VALLEY, MARGARET RIVER, NAPA VALLEY, TUSCANY**

**FAMOUS APPELLATIONS: MARGAUX, PAUILLAC, PESSAC LÉOGNAN, SAINT ESTÈPHE, SAINT-JULIEN**

**SWEETNESS: DRY**

**FRUITS: HIGH**

**ACIDITY: HIGH**

**ALCOHOL: MEDIUM TO HIGH**

**TANNINS: HIGH**

**BODY: FULL**

**GLASSWARE: BIG RED**

**TEMPERATURE: ROOM**

**BUDGET: £–£££**

Cabernet Sauvignon is the result of a spontaneous genetic crossing between Cabernet Franc and Sauvignon Blanc. There are now more hectares of Cabernet Sauvignon planted in the world than any other grape. It thrives in a variety of soils, most famously on the well-drained gravel mounds of Bordeaux. It requires a significant amount of heat to reach ripeness – something that it struggles to achieve consistently in Bordeaux. Although it shows itself differently depending upon location, one can always count on a wine that is identifiable as Cabernet Sauvignon. Blackcurrant is the dominant fruit, along with other black fruits, and the wines also display beautiful notes of mint and black pepper that complement a rich structure based on loads of acidity, body, tannin and alcohol. This is a grape that has great affinity with oak and tremendous ageing potential. With age, Cabernet Sauvignon wines develop aromas of cedar and cigar box.

**STYLES:**
Cabernet Sauvignon is an excellent blending partner. As a blended wine, it plays an important role in Bordeaux, where it is paired with Merlot. It is found in other places as part of the 'Bordeaux blend' or blended with local grapes such as Syrah, Garnacha and Sangiovese. Although it is very uncommon to find Cabernet Sauvignon unblended in Bordeaux, it is produced as a varietal in many wine regions, including California and Tuscany.

**FLAVOURS:**
Blackcurrant, plum, black cherry, blackberry, mint, toast, black pepper

**CELLAR:**
5–20+ years. Wines from top appellations can last for decades.

# PASTEL DE CHOCLO
## [CORN PIE]

**SERVES: 6**

——

**TIME: 90 MINS**

——

FOR THE CORN PASTE:
2 tbsp butter
1 tbsp sunflower oil
1kg frozen sweetcorn
70–100ml whole milk
12 leaves of basil
sea salt and black pepper

FOR THE MEAT FILLING:
2 tbsp sunflower oil
1kg beef mince
3 onions, finely chopped
1 tbsp dried chilli flakes
½ tsp ground cumin
2 tbsp plain flour
500g cooked chicken
   breast, diced
handful of sultanas
200g black olives, pitted
3 hard-boiled eggs, sliced
2–3 tbsp golden caster sugar

I remember going with my mother to the local market to buy fresh corn cobs during the summer in Chile. They were huge! *Pastel de choclo* is an iconic dish back home. This corn pie is an incredible combination of corn paste, beef, chicken, olives, onions, raisins and hard-boiled eggs, with a slightly caramelised crust on the top. It's simply fantastic. You normally eat it with a fresh tomato salad on the side. **Cabernet Sauvignon**-based wines are the best choice to match this recipe owing to the intensity of their flavour, body and structure.

1. Melt the butter with the oil in a large saucepan over a medium heat. Add the corn and cook, stirring, for about 10 minutes until toasted and turning golden. Add the milk and basil and season with salt and pepper, then simmer for another 10 minutes until the corn is tender. With a hand blender, blitz the corn mixture until smooth. Check the seasoning and set aside.

2. Heat the oil for the filling in a large, wide pan over a medium– high heat. Cook the beef mince for about 6–7 minutes, stirring regularly, until well coloured. Add the onions, chilli flakes and cumin, season with salt and pepper and cook for another 10 minutes until the onions have softened. Add the flour and mix well with the meat, allowing it to cook off for a minute or two. Slowly add 120ml water, stirring constantly to avoid lumps. Allow the water to come to the boil and stir until thickened to a coating consistency.

3. Preheat the oven to 200°C/gas 6.

4. Spoon a layer of the mince mixture into a large baking dish, then add the chicken, raisins, black olives and hard-boiled eggs in layers on top. Finish with a layer of the corn paste, making sure it completely covers the other layers. Sprinkle the top with sugar and bake for 45 minutes until golden.

# CARIÑENA [CARIGNAN]

**HOME COUNTRY: SPAIN**
—

**OTHER COUNTRIES:
CHILE, FRANCE, ITALY**
—

**MAIN REGIONS: CATALUNYA,
LANGUEDOC-ROUSSILLON,
MAULE VALLEY, PRIORAT,
SARDINIA**
—

**FAMOUS APPELLATIONS:
CARIGNANO DEL SULCIS,
CARIÑENA, COSTERS
DEL SEGRE, MINERVOIS,
MONTSANT**
—

**SWEETNESS: DRY**
—

**FRUITS: HIGH**
—

**ACIDITY: MEDIUM**
—

**ALCOHOL: MEDIUM TO HIGH**
—

**TANNINS: MEDIUM**
—

**BODY: MEDIUM**
—

**GLASSWARE: RED**
—

**TEMPERATURE: ROOM**
—

**CELLAR: 3–5 YEARS**
—

**BUDGET: £**

Cariñena is particularly fond of hot climates. In the right location, this grape makes a wine that is deeply coloured with an abundance of tannin and acidity. Wines made from old vines are especially successful, as their lower yields lead to an increased concentration of flavours. Frequently this grape is an important part of a blend. Cariñena can be found in various locations in Spain, with exceptionally high-quality examples being produced in Priorat. Carignan, as it is called outside of Spain, is also planted in the south of France, Sardinia in Italy and other regions.

**STYLES:**
Wines produced using Cariñena are generally big and powerful. Using carbonic maceration, a lighter, softer wine can be produced. With old vines, some more than 50 years old, a richer, more complex style is made. Examples of varietal wines exist, but it is most successful as a blended wine. Its most frequent blending partners are Syrah or Grenache. Cariñena is also blended to make very tasty rosé.

**FLAVOURS:**
Strawberry, raspberry, plum, blackberry, prune, liquorice, meat

# CHICKEN QUESADILLAS WITH GUACAMOLE

**SERVES: 2**

——

**TIME: 25 MINS**

——

2 tbsp sunflower oil
1 red onion, thinly sliced
1 red pepper, thinly sliced
½ tsp dried chilli flakes
1 small chicken breast,
   finely chopped
2 large flour tortillas
100g grated mozzarella
sea salt and black pepper
lime wedges, to serve

FOR THE GUACAMOLE:
1 large avocado, peeled
   and pitted
1 large tomato, deseeded
   and finely diced
1 garlic clove, crushed
½ bunch of coriander,
   finely chopped
juice of 1 lime

You don't need to be a chef to make this easy and tasty snack. If you don't fancy chicken, replace it with beef, pork or even prawns. You can be creative! Packed with protein, these quesadillas will definitely satisfy your hunger, and the guacamole is a classic accompaniment that adds a spicy twist. The mix of red and black fruits and spicy notes in **Cariñena** will balance well with the zesty flavours of these quesadillas.

1. Heat 1 tablespoon of the oil in a saucepan over a medium heat. Fry the onion and red pepper for 6–8 minutes until beginning to soften. Add the chilli flakes and season with salt and pepper. Add the chicken and cook for 10 minutes until the meat is cooked through.

2. Meanwhile, to make the guacamole, put the avocado in a bowl and mash with a fork before adding the tomato, garlic and coriander. Season with salt and pepper, squeeze in the juice of 1 lime and mix well.

3. Divide the chicken and vegetables between the tortillas and spread over one half to make a semi-circle of the filling. Top the filling with mozzarella, adding half of the cheese to each tortilla, then fold the empty half of the tortillas over the filling. Brush them with the remaining oil.

4. Heat a large non-stick frying pan over a medium heat. Cook the tortillas for 3 minutes on each side, or until the filling is hot and the cheese has melted.

5. Cut the quesadillas into wedges and serve with the guacamole and lime wedges.

'In the right location, this grape makes a wine that is deeply coloured with an abundance of tannin and acidity'

CARIÑENA & CHICKEN QUESADILLAS WITH GUACAMOLE

# CARMÉNÈRE

**HOME COUNTRY: FRANCE**

—

**OTHER COUNTRIES:
CHILE, ITALY**

—

**MAIN REGIONS: BORDEAUX,
COLCHAGUA, FRIULI, MAIPO
VALLEY, RAPEL VALLEY**

—

**FAMOUS APPELLATIONS:
FRIULI LATISANA, PIAVE**

—

**SWEETNESS: DRY**

—

**FRUITS: MEDIUM TO HIGH**

—

**ACIDITY: LOW TO MEDIUM**

—

**ALCOHOL: MEDIUM**

—

**TANNINS: MEDIUM**

—

**BODY: MEDIUM TO HIGH**

—

**GLASSWARE: RED**

—

**TEMPERATURE: ROOM**

—

**CELLAR: 2–3 YEARS FOR
LIGHT STYLES. 10+ YEARS
FOR TOP WINES.**

—

**BUDGET: £–££**

It is likely that Carménère was brought to Bordeaux by the Romans. Until the phylloxera epidemic hit Bordeaux between 1875 and 1892 – when almost half of Europe's vineyards were devastated – Carménère was a major player in the 'Bordeaux blend'. Nowadays, it is only a minor component. It was introduced to Chile in the 19th century, where it thrives. It is naturally low in acidity, making for a soft round wine with lovely savoury characteristics such as coffee, soy sauce and grilled meat. Due to its low acidity, it blends well with Cabernet Sauvignon, bringing down the acidity and adding savoury notes. This grape also has high levels of sugar, which can produce very intense alcoholic wines.

**STYLES:**
Light, youthful, easy to drink examples are made with just a touch of oak. They showcase black fruits and savoury notes with ripe soft tannins. A richer, more complex style is produced when the wines spend a significant amount of time in oak. These wines are rich, and show fruits such as black plum and blackberry, with additional notes of chocolate and coffee.

**FLAVOURS:**
Cherry, black plum, black cherry, blackberry, coffee, toast, vanilla

# CHORIPAN CON PEBRE
## [SPICY HOT DOGS WITH CHILEAN SALSA]

**SERVES: 4**

—

**TIME: 30 MINS**

—

FOR THE CHORIPAN:
8 good-quality spicy
   sausages (fresh chorizo
   would work well)
1 tbsp olive oil
8 hotdog buns

FOR THE PEBRE:
4 tomatoes, deseeded and
   very finely diced
1 garlic clove, crushed
juice of ½ lemon
a small bunch of coriander,
   finely chopped
1 large red chilli, deseeded
   and very finely chopped
1 tbsp extra virgin olive oil
sea salt and black pepper

This is one of the quintessential street food snacks found in Chile, but it's also very common in Argentina and Uruguay. The key is to use excellent quality, firm sausage with plenty of flavour. *Pebre*, a spicy tomato salsa, is an accompaniment to many dishes in South America. The black plum and blackberry notes of a gutsy **Carménère** from Chile are a heavenly match.

1.  Preheat the oven to 190°C/gas 5.

2.  Place the sausages on a baking tray and rub with a little olive oil. Bake for 20–30 minutes until cooked through and deeply golden.

3.  Meanwhile, make the pebre by combining all the ingredients in a bowl. Season well with salt and pepper.

4.  Five minutes before the sausages are cooked, split the buns and place in the oven to toast.

5.  To serve, put each sausage in a bun and top with pebre.

'Carménère is naturally low in acidity, making for a soft round wine with lovely savoury characteristics such as coffee, soy sauce and grilled meat'

CARMÉNÈRE WITH CHORIPAN CON PEBRE

# CORVINA

**HOME COUNTRY: ITALY**

**OTHER COUNTRIES: ARGENTINA, AUSTRALIA**

**MAIN REGIONS: VENETO**

**FAMOUS APPELLATIONS: AMARONE DELLA VALPOLICELLA, BARDOLINO, RECIOTO DELLA VALPOLICELLA, VALPOLICELLA**

**SWEETNESS: DRY TO SWEET**

**FRUITS: MEDIUM TO HIGH**

**ACIDITY: HIGH**

**ALCOHOL: MEDIUM TO HIGH**

**TANNINS: MEDIUM TO HIGH**

**BODY: MEDIUM TO FULL**

**GLASSWARE: RED**

**TEMPERATURE: ROOM**

**CELLAR: 2–3 YEARS FOR YOUNG WINES. 15–20+ YEARS FOR AMARONE DELLA VALPOLICELLA.**

**BUDGET: £–£££**

Corvina is the primary grape for making both Bardolino and Valpolicella wines in northern Italy. The grape is chock-full of acidity and has some lovely aromas. On the nose and palate one finds loads of cherries and floral notes. What the grape lacks is colour and tannin. This grape is used to produce a variety of styles of wine, but truly shines when used to make the rich wine Amarone. For Amarone della Valpolicella, the grapes are air-dried (appassimento technique), which concentrates the sugars, flavours and acids. This creates an intense dry, full-bodied wine with a lot of complexity.

**STYLES:**
Light styles of wine are made in which the aromas of sour cherry are evident and the wines are easily quaffed. Amarone della Valpolicella is a much more complex wine thanks to the use of air-dried grapes. A delicious sweet wine, called Recioto della Valpolicella, can also be made using the same blend of grapes and drying technique.

**FLAVOURS:**
Sour cherry, strawberry, cranberry, black plum, black cherry, raisin, toast

# PARMA HAM-WRAPPED PORK

**SERVES: 4**

—

**TIME: 45 MINS**

—

2 tbsp Dijon mustard
2 tbsp honey
10 slices Parma ham
2 pork tenderloins, each
    about 300–350g
1 tbsp oil
500g baby potatoes
250g cherry tomatoes, halved
1 tbsp dried thyme
sea salt and black pepper

This recipe looks very elegant on the plate, but isn't difficult to make. The pork tenderloin is balanced by the cured, salty Parma ham. Serve it warm as a main course or cold at aperitif time. Pair with a wine from the Veneto region – either a light Valpolicella or the much richer, complex Amarone. Both are made with **Corvina** grapes, either will suit this dish well.

1. Preheat the oven to 200°C/gas 6.

2. Mix the mustard with the honey in a small bowl.

3. Lay out 2 large sheets of clingfilm and on each one lay 5 slices of Parma ham, overlapping slightly along their length. Place one tenderloin on top of each Parma ham blanket.

4. Brush each tenderloin with the mustard and honey mixture and season with salt and pepper. Carefully roll up each tenderloin using the cling film to help you roll as tightly as possible. Discard the clingfilm.

5. Heat the oil in an ovenproof large frying pan and carefully add the wrapped tenderloins to brown on all sides. Transfer the pan to the oven and roast for 20 minutes, or until the pork is cooked through. Remove from the oven, cover with foil and let rest for 10 minutes in the pan before cutting.

6. Meanwhile, cook the new potatoes in boiling water until tender, about 15 minutes. Once cooked, drain the pan and add the tomatoes and thyme, and season with salt.

7. Cut the tenderloin rolls on a diagonal into thick slices and serve with the vegetables.

# GAMAY

**HOME COUNTRY: FRANCE**

**OTHER COUNTRIES: CROATIA, SERBIA, SWITZERLAND**

**MAIN REGIONS: BEAUJOLAIS, LOIRE**

**FAMOUS APPELLATIONS: BROUILLY, FLEURIE, JULIENAS, MORGON, MOULIN-À-VENT**

**SWEETNESS: DRY**

**FRUITS: MEDIUM TO HIGH**

**ACIDITY: MEDIUM TO HIGH**

**ALCOHOL: MEDIUM**

**TANNINS: LOW**

**BODY: LIGHT TO MEDIUM**

**GLASSWARE: RED**

**TEMPERATURE: ROOM OR LIGHTLY CHILLED**

**CELLAR: 3–10 YEARS**

**BUDGET: £–££**

Gamay is a grape that is found almost exclusively in the region of Beaujolais in France. It makes an underrated, lovely wine with delicious red fruits (raspberries and cherries), a flinty minerality, and a touch of peppery spice. It is delicate, has a pale ruby colour, low tannins and low to medium acidity. The best examples of Beaujolais come from the ten Cru villages, which are found on granite hills in the northern part of the region. Delicious wines are also being produced by the 39 villages that also sit on granite soils and may label their wines as Beaujolais-Villages. In the southern, flatter part of the region, 'basic' Beaujolais is made, which is a more simple, softer wine. Here, many producers use a method called carbonic maceration which contributes to their wines' soft profile.

**STYLES:**
Light, fresh styles of Beaujolais are simple wines with some red fruits and are generally unoaked. Complex examples come from the granite hills (from the Crus or Beaujolais-Villages). These wines have seen some oak and display a wide range of ripe red fruits and a flinty minerality.

**FLAVOURS:**
Cherry, strawberry, raspberry, cranberry, banana, bubblegum

# SPICED POTATO CHIPS

**SERVES: 6**

—

**TIME: 60 MINS**

—

**VEGETARIAN**

—

5 tbsp olive oil
½ tsp dried chilli flakes
1 tbsp smoked paprika
½ tsp dried thyme
2 garlic cloves, crushed
600g potatoes, peeled,
   sliced into 1cm thick chips
600g sweet potatoes,
   peeled, sliced into 1cm
   thick chips
sea salt
Tzatziki (see page 41),
   to serve

This simple recipe makes a great snack in the afternoon or before dinner. Sweet potato chips have become quite popular. Here, I mix ordinary and sweet potatoes, enjoying the different flavours and colours that each potato brings to the mix. They are fantastic served piping hot, but are also tasty cold. Wines made with **Gamay** are low in tannins and show delicious red fruits and a hint of spiciness, making them a perfect match with the potato chips.

1.  Preheat the oven to 200°C/gas 6.

2.  Mix the olive oil with the chilli, paprika, thyme, garlic and salt to taste.

3.  Spread the potatoes out on a large baking tray and spread the sweet potatoes out on a second large tray. Drizzle the spiced oil over both trays and toss gently to coat. Put the tray of standard potatoes in the oven and roast for 25 minutes. After this time add the sweet potato tray to the oven and continue roasting both trays for another 20–25 minutes. Carefully turn all the potatoes a few times during cooking so that they become evenly crisp and golden on the outside and soft in the middle.

4.  Transfer the cooked chips to serving bowls, sprinkle with a little more sea salt and serve with tzatziki for dipping.

# GARNACHA [GRENACHE]

**HOME COUNTRY: SPAIN**

**OTHER COUNTRIES: AUSTRALIA, FRANCE, ITALY**

**MAIN REGIONS: PRIORAT, RHÔNE VALLEY, SARDINIA**

**FAMOUS APPELLATIONS: CANNONAU DI SARDEGNA, CHÂTEAUNEUF-DU-PAPE, CÔTES DU RHÔNE, MINERVOIS, NAVARRA, PRIORAT, RIOJA**

**SWEETNESS: DRY TO SWEET**

**FRUITS: HIGH**

**ACIDITY: MEDIUM**

**ALCOHOL: MEDIUM TO HIGH**

**TANNINS: MEDIUM**

**BODY: MEDIUM TO HIGH**

**GLASSWARE: RED**

**TEMPERATURE: ROOM**

**CELLAR: 5–10 YEARS**

**BUDGET: £–££**

Garnacha (or Grenache in France) thrives in hot, dry locations. Full of delicious strawberry fruits, it packs a real punch with high alcohol. Old vines in Priorat and other areas of Spain make wines with amazing depth and complexity. Grenache also grows quite happily in the southern Rhône. It is a versatile grape that can produce wines of various styles – from light to full bodied, and even sweet wines. It is commonly used in France and Spain as part of a blend for rosé wines.

**STYLES:**
Light style wines are easy to drink with refreshing acidity. They fill the mouth with fresh strawberries, hints of other red fruits and perhaps a little earth or leather. Older vines and smaller yields allow for more complex wines that have great ability to age. These wines have the potential for a variety of aromas: concentrated fruits, spices, coffee, leather, roasted nuts and more.

**FLAVOURS:**
Cherry, strawberry, raspberry, black cherry, black pepper, leather

# CHICKPEAS WITH CHORIZO

**SERVES: 4**

—

**TIME: 30 MINS**

—

2 tbsp olive oil

200g chorizo, roughly
chopped

1 red onion, thinly sliced

1 red pepper, finely chopped

4 celery sticks, finely sliced

1 large carrot, peeled and
finely diced

2 x 400g tins chickpeas,
drained and rinsed

1 x 400g tin chopped
tomatoes

a bunch of coriander,
finely chopped

sea salt and black pepper

This is a recipe that I prepare frequently. Chickpeas with chorizo is inspired by ingredients from southern Spain. The chorizo adds spice and the chickpeas have a pleasing, chewy texture and are a great source of fibre and protein. The addition of the other vegetables makes for a nice blend of different flavours and textures. **Garnacha**, one of my favourite black grapes, is an excellent choice with this dish. The red fruit flavours and spicy notes will complement the recipe well.

1. Heat the olive oil in a large saucepan over a medium heat. Add the chorizo and fry gently to release the oils and give it some colour. Remove from the pan with a slotted spoon, leaving the oil in the pan, and set aside.

2. Add the onion, red pepper, celery and carrot to the chorizo oil in the pan. Season with salt and black pepper and cook for 10 minutes until the vegetables are softened.

3. Return the chorizo to the pan along with the chickpeas and tomatoes. Add 100ml water and cook for another 10 minutes until you have a slightly thickened sauce. Stir through most of the coriander, then taste and adjust the seasoning.

4. Sprinkle with the remaining coriander to serve.

'These wines have the potential for a variety of aromas: concentrated fruits, spices, coffee, leather, roasted nuts and more'

GARNACHA & CHICKPEAS WITH CHORIZO

# MALBEC

**HOME COUNTRY: FRANCE**

**OTHER COUNTRIES:
ARGENTINA, CHILE**

**MAIN REGIONS: BORDEAUX,
CAHORS, CENTRAL VALLEY,
MENDOZA**

**FAMOUS APPELLATIONS:
CAHORS**

**SWEETNESS: DRY**

**FRUITS: HIGH**

**ACIDITY: MEDIUM**

**ALCOHOL: MEDIUM TO HIGH**

**TANNINS: MEDIUM TO HIGH**

**BODY: MEDIUM TO HIGH**

**GLASSWARE: RED**

**TEMPERATURE: ROOM**

**CELLAR: 2–3 YEARS FOR
YOUNG STYLES. 10+ YEARS
FOR TOP WINES.**

**BUDGET: £–££**

Malbec is native to southwest France, but has truly made a name for itself in Argentina. Here, it shows off its soft, round, ripe juicy character. The best examples in Argentina are made from vines grown at an altitude of around 1,000 metres and higher. These wines have seductive, lush ripe tannins, black fruits and aromas of violet and chocolate. In France, Bordeaux was Malbec's homeland, but now the grape is identified with Cahors, a region in the southwest, where very dense, deep coloured wines with a minimum of 70 per cent Malbec are produced. These wines tend towards flavours of black plums, raisins and tobacco.

**STYLES:**
Simple wines are made to be drunk young. They have spent little time in oak and with their refreshing acidity and soft ripe tannins are easy to drink. The more complex wines, using grapes grown at altitude in Argentina, are built to age. These wines will see much more significant oak treatment, riper fruit flavours, aromas of violets, and possess lush tannins balanced by good acidity.

**FLAVOURS:**
Plum, black cherry, blackberry, black pepper, vanilla, toast

# CHURRASCO
## [STEAK SANDWICH]

**SERVES: 2**

———

**TIME: 20 MINS**

———

300g rib-eye steak
1 tbsp olive oil
2 ciabatta rolls
1 avocado, peeled and pitted
2 tbsp mayonnaise
1 ripe tomato, sliced
½ tsp dried chilli flakes
    (optional)
sea salt and black pepper

The Chileans are obsessed with sandwiches! There are many places in Chile specifically dedicated to the serious and delicious business of serving sandwiches. When I was at school, I remember frequently enjoying freshly made *churrascos* with my mates. The taste was always great and I appreciated the fact that it only cost a couple of pounds. A young, fruit-forward **Malbec** with its refreshing acidity is an incredible match for a steak-based sandwich.

1. Preheat the oven to 180°C/gas 4.

2. Season the steak with salt and pepper and rub the olive oil all over it. Leave it at room temperature for 15 minutes.

3. Heat a frying pan over a high heat and, once hot, place the steak in the centre of the pan. Cook for 3 minutes on each side for medium. Remove the steak from the pan and allow to rest for 5 minutes.

4. While the steak is resting, warm the ciabatta rolls in the oven for 5 minutes. Put the avocado in a bowl and mash with a fork to a chunky purée.

5. Cut open the rolls and spread the avocado purée on one side. On the other side, spread the mayonnaise, then add the tomato slices.

6. Slice the steak as thinly as possible and divide it between the rolls. Add a sprinkle of chilli flakes if you fancy your churrasco a bit spicier. Sandwich the two sides of the roll together and serve.

# MERLOT

**HOME COUNTRY: FRANCE**

—

**OTHER COUNTRIES: AUSTRALIA, CHILE, ITALY, USA**

—

**MAIN REGIONS: BORDEAUX, MAIPO VALLEY, MARGARET RIVER, NAPA VALLEY, TUSCANY**

—

**FAMOUS APPELLATIONS: POMEROL, SAINT-ÉMILION, VENETO**

—

**SWEETNESS: DRY**

—

**FRUITS: HIGH**

—

**ACIDITY: MEDIUM**

—

**ALCOHOL: MEDIUM TO HIGH**

—

**TANNINS: MEDIUM**

—

**BODY: MEDIUM TO HIGH**

—

**GLASSWARE: RED**

—

**TEMPERATURE: ROOM**

—

**CELLAR: 5–20+ YEARS**

—

**BUDGET: £–£££**

Merlot is purported to be named after the blackbird (*merle* in French), who is quite fond of the sweet Merlot berries. This grape is widely planted throughout the world, although its homeland is France where it is the most-planted grape. This is a difficult grape to pin down as it can range from juicy and light to ripe with lots of texture and body. It stands on its own as a varietal wine and is a regular blending partner thanks to its flexible characteristics. In the 'Bordeaux blend' it is added to soften tannins, moderate acidity and add a complexity of flavours.

**STYLES:**
Varietal wines made using only Merlot are most often described as 'velvety'. They are 'smooth' and easy to drink, with a mix of red and/or black fruits and an array of other aromas, such as liquorice, tobacco, and cinnamon. As part of a blend, it helps to make wines that are rich in style, have intense black and red fruit character, noticeable oak, and a seemingly endless list of possible aromas. These wines have great ageing potential.

**FLAVOURS:**
Red plum, cherry, strawberry, black cherry, prune, cloves, toast, vanilla

# SPICY SCRAMBLED EGGS

**SERVES: 2**

———

**TIME: 15 MINS**

———

**VEGETARIAN**

———

2 tbsp olive oil
½ red onion, finely chopped
1 red pepper, deseeded and
    finely chopped
1 green pepper, deseeded
    and finely chopped
250g cherry tomatoes, halved
1 garlic clove, crushed
½ tsp dried chilli flakes
½ tsp dried thyme
4 eggs, lightly beaten
½ bunch of coriander,
    roughly chopped
sea salt and black pepper
2–4 slices of sourdough bread,
    toasted, to serve

Here's a great suggestion for a weekend brunch. Paired with some freshly made bread, an assortment of fruits with yoghurt and a glass of wine, you've got the makings of a special weekend meal. These eggs would even work well as an easy weekday dinner. **Merlot** produces some powerful wines with great ageing potential, as well as some very fruit-driven easy drinking styles that would be perfect for sipping alongside this egg dish.

1. Heat the oil in a large frying pan over a medium heat. Add the onion and peppers, and cook until the onion is translucent and the peppers are tender, about 8–10 minutes.

2. Add the cherry tomatoes, and cook for a further 2–3 minutes before adding the garlic, chilli flakes and thyme. Season with salt and black pepper and cook for another minute or so.

3. Once the vegetables are soft, turn down the heat to low and add the eggs. Cook them for 1–2 minutes, stirring gently, until just beginning to set, being very careful not to overcook them. Check the seasoning and stir in the coriander.

4. Serve the scrambled eggs with toasted bread.

# MONASTRELL [MOURVÈDRE]

**HOME COUNTRY: SPAIN**

**OTHER COUNTRIES: AUSTRALIA, FRANCE, USA**

**MAIN REGIONS: BAROSSA VALLEY, CATALUNYA, LANGUEDOC-ROUSSILLON, MURCIA, NAPA VALLEY, RHÔNE VALLEY, VALENCIA**

**FAMOUS APPELLATIONS: BANDOL, CATALUNYA, CÔTES DU RHÔNE, JUMILLA, VALENCIA, YECLA**

**SWEETNESS: DRY**

**FRUITS: MEDIUM TO HIGH**

**ACIDITY: MEDIUM**

**ALCOHOL: MEDIUM TO HIGH**

**TANNINS: HIGH**

**BODY: FULL**

**GLASSWARE: RED**

**TEMPERATURE: ROOM**

**CELLAR: 7–10 YEARS**

**BUDGET: £–££**

Monastrell is an old grape variety that originated in the medieval city of Murviedro, near Valencia. Not surprisingly, most are familiar with its French name, Mourvèdre, as it is found in the southern Rhône and on the Mediterranean coast where it thrives. Bandol is a famous appellation in France that needs to have a minimum of 50 per cent of Mourvèdre in the blend. In Australia and California it frequently goes by the name Mataró. In Spain, it is popular in the regions of Valencia and Catalunya. With Monastrell one can count on a wine with its fair share of tannins and alcohol.

**STYLES:**
Whether as a single varietal or more commonly as part of a blended wine, Monastrell will make a dense wine with complex aromas of herbs, farmyard and ripe blackberry fruits.

**FLAVOURS:**
Red plum, cherry, blackberry, black pepper, herbs, game, leather

# CAZUELA DE POLLO
## [CHICKEN SOUP]

**SERVES: 4**

—

**TIME: 1 HOUR**

—

2 tbsp olive oil
1 onion, finely diced
1 red pepper, finely diced
2 carrots, peeled: 1 finely
   diced, 1 thickly sliced
1 garlic clove, crushed
4 chicken thighs, skin on
   and bone in
500ml chicken stock
200g baby potatoes,
   scrubbed
200g pumpkin flesh,
   cut into large dice
3 cobs of corn, each cut
   into 3 pieces
150g long grain rice
½ bunch of coriander,
   finely chopped
sea salt and black pepper

*Cazuela de pollo* is a traditional chicken soup that is featured on every menu in Chile. It works equally well for lunch or dinner and it will warm you up in the winter months. **Monastrell** has flavours and structure that will enhance the flavours of this delectable dish.

1. Heat the olive oil in a large saucepan over a medium heat and add the onion, pepper and diced carrot. Cook for about 8–10 minutes, or until the vegetables are tender, then stir in the garlic. Add the chicken and season with salt and black pepper.

2. Add the chicken stock and 500ml water, along with the potatoes and sliced carrot. Bring the liquid to the boil, then lower the heat to a gentle simmer, cover with a lid and cook for 10 minutes, occasionally skimming away the fat if necessary. Add the pumpkin, corn and rice and cook for another 10–15 minutes, or until the chicken, rice and vegetables are cooked through.

3. Put some chopped coriander in each of four bowls and ladle in the soup, making sure each bowl receives a piece of chicken, some potatoes, pumpkin and corn. Sprinkle with more coriander and serve.

'Monastrell makes a dense wine with complex aromas of herbs, farmyard and ripe blackberry fruits'

MONASTRELL WITH CAZUELA DE POLLO

# MONTEPULCIANO

**HOME COUNTRY: ITALY**

**OTHER COUNTRIES: AUSTRALIA, NEW ZEALAND, USA**

**MAIN REGIONS: ABRUZZO, MARCHE, MOLISE**

**FAMOUS APPELLATIONS: COLLINE TERAMANE MONTEPULCIANO D'ABRUZZO, MONTEPULCIANO D'ABRUZZO, ROSSO CONERO, ROSSO PICENO**

**SWEETNESS: DRY**

**FRUITS: MEDIUM**

**ACIDITY: MEDIUM TO HIGH**

**ALCOHOL: MEDIUM**

**TANNINS: MEDIUM TO HIGH**

**BODY: MEDIUM TO HIGH**

**GLASSWARE: RED**

**TEMPERATURE: ROOM**

**CELLAR: 3–5 YEARS**

**BUDGET: £**

Montepulciano is an extremely popular grape in Italy and is the second most planted behind Sangiovese. It can be found in no fewer than 40 of the DOC and DOCG regions in Italy. Its homeland of Abruzzo, the region east of Rome, produces an abundance of easy-to-drink wines. Some of the best are found in the Colline Teramane foothills. Montepulciano performs equally well as a blending partner or as a single variety. Expect wines with a mix of red fruits and blackberries, deep colour and round, soft tannins. In Italy, this is a great go-to grape for good-value wines.

**STYLES:**
The most simple and easy to drink wines are unoaked. These examples deliver fresh red and black fruits. Riper fruit is often fermented or aged in oak, producing a richer wine with more diverse flavours and soft tannins.

**FLAVOURS:**
Cherry, strawberry, red plum, blackberry, black pepper, herbs, toast, prune

# AREPAS WITH REINA PEPIADA

**SERVES: 4**

———

**TIME: 30 MINS**

———

FOR THE AREPAS:
1 tsp sea salt
250g white maize flour
   (Harina Pan is the best
   brand for this recipe)
2 tbsp sunflower oil

FOR THE REINA PEPIADA:
1 avocado, peeled and pitted
250g leftover cooked chicken
   or rotisserie chicken,
   shredded
1 tbsp mayonnaise
a squeeze of lime juice
a small bunch of coriander,
   finely chopped
sea salt and black pepper

When I was a young child, my family lived in Venezuela for several years. The most quintessential dish of Venezuela is *arepa*. This fried cornbread has an extraordinary combination of textures; soft inside and crunchy on the outside. It can be served with a huge variety of fillings, of which the *reina pepiada* (avocado mash and chicken) is the most iconic. The ripe black fruits of **Montepulciano** make it a great pairing for this enjoyable snack.

1. Put the salt and 425ml water in a mixing bowl. Add the maize flour in a slow, steady stream, stirring constantly to combine. Don't add the flour too quickly or you may get lumps. Allow to stand for 5 minutes for the water to be absorbed.

2. When it's hydrated, use your hands to knead for a few minutes until you get a soft, slightly sticky but malleable dough. Divide the dough into 8 evenly-sized balls, then flatten each ball into a small disc about 1.5cm thick. These are your arepas! Let them rest for 5 minutes while you put together the reina pepiada.

3. Put the avocado in a bowl and mash with a fork. Add the chicken, mayonnaise, lime juice and the coriander. Season and mix well.

4. Heat 1 tablespoon of the oil in a non-stick frying pan over a medium heat and place 4 arepas in the pan. Cover and cook for 6–8 minutes, then uncover, flip the arepas and cook for another 6–8 minutes on the other side. You are looking for them to be cooked through with a golden shell; a bit of charring in places is good. Remove the arepas to a plate lined with kitchen towel, and add another 1 tablespoon of oil to the pan to cook the second batch in the same way.

5. Once they're all cooked and slightly cooled, slice open each arepa along one side, creating a pocket, and fill them with the reina pepiada.

'Expect wines with a mix
of red fruits and blackberries,
deep colour and round,
soft tannins'

MONTEPULCIANO & AREPAS WITH REINA PEPIADA

# NEBBIOLO

**HOME COUNTRY: ITALY**

**OTHER COUNTRIES: ARGENTINA, AUSTRALIA, USA**

**MAIN REGIONS: LOMBARDY, PIEDMONT**

**FAMOUS APPELLATIONS: BARBARESCO, BAROLO, CAREMA, FRANCIACORTA, GATTINARA, LANGHE, ROERO, VALTELLINA**

**SWEETNESS: DRY**

**FRUITS: MEDIUM TO HIGH**

**ACIDITY: HIGH**

**ALCOHOL: HIGH**

**TANNINS: HIGH**

**BODY: FULL**

**GLASSWARE: RED**

**TEMPERATURE: ROOM**

**CELLAR: 10–20+ YEARS**

**BUDGET: £££**

Nebbiolo's history has not been confirmed, but most experts believe that it is native to Piedmont. Although Barbera is much more widely planted in the region, it is Nebbiolo that garners most of the prestige. It does best on the steep clay and limestone slopes of Piedmont, yet, it is a grape that adapts to many soils and displays different traits depending on where it is grown. It does not lack acidity or tannin and can show off some of the most interesting aromas of any grape variety. Initially this is intense with red fruits but there are also floral notes, such as rose and violet. Young wines are a gorgeous pale ruby colour and age gracefully to an even more stunning garnet (brick) colour.

**STYLES:**
When it comes to young wines, it is easy to pick out the red fruits, including cherries and plums, and identify some floral aromas. But, it is with some age that the wines really come into their own and show amazing complexity. These wines have an intriguing profile of red fruits, floral notes, dried herbs, leather, tar and spice. With maturity, the tannins also soften to add a velvety texture.

**FLAVOURS:**
Cherry, plum, strawberry, raspberry, cranberry, rose, violets, leather, herbs, liquorice

# FRIED AUBERGINES WITH HONEY

**SERVES: 4**

———

**TIME: 30 MINS**

———

**VEGETARIAN**

———

2 aubergines, cut into
  1cm thick disks
5 tbsp olive oil
plain flour, for dredging
honey, for drizzling
sea salt and black pepper

Andalucia, in the south of Spain, has a rich cultural and culinary heritage. This recipe echoes the strong Moorish influence in the area, and is found especially around Malaga and Granada. It is traditionally made with *miel de caña*, which translates as 'sugar cane honey' but is commonly known as molasses. Here, I used a good-quality honey instead of *miel de caña* which works equally well. **Nebbiolo**'s high acidity matches perfectly with the fried aubergines, as with other fried dishes.

1. Put the aubergine slices on a large tray and lightly salt each one on both sides. Leave for 20 minutes, then pat both sides dry with kitchen towel.

2. Heat the oil in a large frying pan over a medium heat.

3. Put some flour onto a plate, season with salt and pepper and mix well. Dredge the aubergine slices in the flour, then turn over and coat the other sides.

4. Using tongs, lift the aubergine slices from the plate and shake them a bit to remove any excess flour before putting them in the hot oil. Cook for 1–2 minutes until golden brown, then flip over and cook for another minute on the other side. You will need to do this in batches so you don't overcrowd the pan.

5. Once cooked, remove the aubergines with the tongs and place them on a large tray lined with kitchen towel to drain.

6. To serve, arrange the aubergine slices on a large serving dish. Add a scattering of salt and drizzle lots of honey on top.

'Initially Nebbiolo is intense with red fruits but there are also floral notes, such as rose and violet'

NEBBIOLO & FRIED AUBERGINES WITH HONEY

# NERO D'AVOLA

**HOME COUNTRY: ITALY**

**OTHER COUNTRIES: AUSTRALIA, USA**

**MAIN REGIONS: SICILY**

**FAMOUS APPELLATIONS: CERASUOLO DI VITTORIA, NOTO, PACHINO, SICILIA**

**SWEETNESS: DRY**

**FRUITS: HIGH**

**ACIDITY: MEDIUM TO HIGH**

**ALCOHOL: MEDIUM TO HIGH**

**TANNINS: HIGH**

**BODY: FULL**

**GLASSWARE: RED**

**TEMPERATURE: ROOM**

**CELLAR: 5–10 YEARS**

**BUDGET: £–££**

Nero d'Avola is indigenous to Sicily and one of its most well-known grapes. The grape thrives in the island's warm climate. The wines produced are redolent of red and black fruits, spice with a hint of floral character. Nero d'Avola lacks neither body nor tannins but the wines it makes are still delicious drunk young. The grape responds well to judicious use of oak and after some years in bottle maintains flavour and interest. Since the Middle Ages, this grape has been used to boost colour and add texture to lighter-style wines in the rest of Italy.

**STYLES:**
Unoaked, these easy-to-drink wines are fresh with a mix of red and black fruits. When some oak is introduced, the tannins are softer and more integrated, but the wines still display an array of fruits and floral aromas. The wines have some potential to age.

**FLAVOURS:**
Cherry, strawberry, black plum, black cherry, blackberry, tobacco, prune

# PICHANGA

**SERVES: 6**

——

**TIME: 20 MINS**

——

250g ham, diced
250g Gouda, diced
250g good-quality
   mortadella, diced
250g pitted olives
   (a variety of types)
250g assorted pickled
   vegetables, such as
   gherkins, onions, carrots
   and cauliflower
½ tsp dried chilli flakes
1 loaf of focaccia bread,
   to serve

*Pichanga*, the name of this Chilean recipe, has a double meaning – and both meanings bring a smile to my face. The most obvious translation is that it's the name of this beloved recipe. But secondly, 'pichanga de barrio' is a football game that my friends and I played on the street as children. *Pichanga* is best enjoyed with a glass of wine or a beer. The boldness of **Nero d'Avola** stands up to the lively flavours of pickles, chilli and Gouda in this tasty appetiser.

1.  This is very simple. Mix all the ingredients, except the bread, in a large bowl.

2.  Add all the juice from the jar of pickled vegetables. Cover the bowl with a lid or clingfilm and put in the fridge for 10 minutes.

3.  Serve the pichanga with warm focaccia bread.

# PINOT NOIR

**HOME COUNTRY: FRANCE**

**OTHER COUNTRIES: GERMANY, NEW ZEALAND, USA**

**MAIN REGIONS: BADEN, BURGUNDY, CENTRAL OTAGO, CHAMPAGNE, OREGON, PFALZ**

**FAMOUS APPELLATIONS: BEAUNE, GEVRY-CHAMBERTIN, NUITS-SAINT-GEORGES, POMMARD**

**SWEETNESS: DRY**

**FRUITS: MEDIUM TO HIGH**

**ACIDITY: HIGH**

**ALCOHOL: MEDIUM**

**TANNINS: LIGHT TO MEDIUM**

**BODY: LIGHT TO MEDIUM**

**GLASSWARE: RED**

**TEMPERATURE: ROOM OR LIGHTLY CHILLED**

**CELLAR: 2-3 YEARS. TOP WINES CAN AGE FOR DECADES.**

**BUDGET: ££-£££**

Pinot Noir, one of the most ancient grape varieties in the world, is thought to have already existed in Burgundy prior to the arrival of the Romans. It is the grape that produces some of the most celebrated, and costly, wines in the world – red burgundy. More than 15 grape varieties lay claim to Pinot Noir as one of its parents. This is a rather delicate grape, but in the right place it is one of the most expressive grapes that exists. In cool to moderate climate regions like Central Otago and Oregon, Pinot Noir thrives, producing wines with high acidity, red fruit flavours and typical savoury notes of earth, mushroom, game and leather.

**STYLES:**
Successful Pinot Noir is always fresh in style, but they can range from simple and easy to drink to the better, more complex, wines with loads of aromas and structure. Rosé wines are also made with this thin-skinned grape. Some sparkling wines, for example champagne, can be made using Pinot Noir.

**FLAVOURS:**
Cherry, strawberry, raspberry, cranberry, game, mushroom, leather, toast

# SAGANAKI

2 tbsp sunflower oil
1 egg
200g piece of feta, halloumi
  or manouri cheese
plain flour, to coat
1 tbsp toasted sesame seeds
a drizzle of honey
1 lemon, cut into wedges

*Saganaki* is a Greek recipe and the word simply means 'fried cheese'. This recipe is extremely popular in the Greek tavernas. I am a huge fan of feta – I particularly love the texture, saltiness and strong flavour. And then, imagine it fried! The high acidity and red fruits of **Pinot Noir** are a perfect foil to the crispy crust and tangy cheese of the *saganaki*.

1. Heat the oil in a non-stick frying pan over a medium heat.

2. Meanwhile, beat the egg in a large glass bowl. Dip the entire piece of cheese in the egg, then very carefully coat it lightly with flour, making sure you don't break the piece of cheese.

3. Put the cheese in the hot pan and cook for 2 minutes on each side until it is golden-brown. Carefully remove it from the pan and place on some kitchen towel to absorb the oil.

4. Put the cheese on a serving plate and scatter over the toasted sesame seeds. Drizzle over some honey and garnish with lemon wedges for squeezing over.

'The high acidity and red fruits of Pinot Noir are a perfect foil to the crispy crust and tangy cheese of the saganaki'

PINOT NOIR WITH SAGANAKI

# PRIMITIVO [ZINFANDEL]

**HOME COUNTRY: CROATIA**

**OTHER COUNTRIES: ITALY, USA**

**MAIN REGIONS: NAPA VALLEY, PUGLIA**

**FAMOUS APPELLATIONS: FALERNO DEL MASSICO PRIMITIVO, GIOIA DEL COLLE PRIMITIVO, PRIMITIVO DI MANDURIA**

**SWEETNESS: DRY**

**FRUITS: HIGH**

**ACIDITY: MEDIUM**

**ALCOHOL: HIGH**

**TANNINS: MEDIUM**

**BODY: FULL**

**GLASSWARE: RED**

**TEMPERATURE: ROOM**

**CELLAR: 5–8 YEARS**

**BUDGET: £–££**

Primitivo originated in Croatia, where it is called *Crljenak kaštelanski*. From there the grape made its way to Italy and California. In California, where it is called Zinfandel, it is very important as a varietal wine. In New World examples, look for jammy fruits and notes of spice. Primitivo produces big wines with lots of tannin, deep colour, intense fruit flavours and high alcohol.

**STYLES:**
A fresh style Primitivo is made in the region of Puglia, the 'heel' of southern Italy. These wines have a mix of red and black fruits and an intense floral character. In California, as Zinfandel, the grape flourishes and produces a much richer style. California wines are brimming with jammy fruits, spice and chocolate.

**FLAVOURS:**
Cherry, strawberry, blackcurrant, black cherry, raisin, prunes, toast, vanilla

# POROTOS GRANADOS
## [CHILEAN BEAN STEW]

**SERVES: 4**

---

**TIME: 35 MINS**

---

**VEGETARIAN**

---

1 tbsp olive oil
1 onion, finely chopped
1 tsp smoked paprika
250g pumpkin flesh, diced
250g sweetcorn kernels (fresh if possible, otherwise frozen)
3 tomatoes, deseeded and diced
2 x 400g tins cannellini beans, drained and rinsed
500ml vegetable stock
6–8 basil leaves, roughly chopped

This summer recipe, featuring pumpkin, cannellini beans and corn, comes from Chile. It's thought of as a summer stew because it's during the summer that corn and pumpkins are harvested there. This is another dish that actually tastes better the day after it's made, allowing the flavours to develop and meld together. The jammy fruits of **Primitivo** pair especially well with the sweet flavour of pumpkin and corn.

1. Heat the oil in a large saucepan over a medium heat. Add the onion and cook for 8–10 minutes, until golden and soft, then add the paprika and cook for a further 1 minute.

2. Add the pumpkin, corn, tomatoes, cannellini beans and the vegetable stock, then season with salt and black pepper. Stir and check the seasoning, then cook, covered, for 25 minutes until everything is tender.

3. Add the basil leaves just before serving.

# SANGIOVESE

**HOME COUNTRY: ITALY**

**OTHER COUNTRIES:**
**ARGENTINA, ROMANIA, USA**

**MAIN REGIONS: EMILIA**
**ROMAGNA, MARCHE,**
**TUSCANY**

**FAMOUS APPELLATIONS:**
**BRUNELLO DI MONTALCINO,**
**CHIANTI, TOSCANA**
**IGT, VINO NOBILE DI**
**MONTEPULCIANO**

**SWEETNESS: DRY**

**FRUITS: MEDIUM**

**ACIDITY: HIGH**

**ALCOHOL: MEDIUM TO HIGH**

**TANNINS: MEDIUM TO HIGH**

**BODY: MEDIUM TO HIGH**

**GLASSWARE: RED**

**TEMPERATURE: ROOM**

**CELLAR: 5–15+ YEARS.**
**PREMIUM WINES CAN AGE**
**FOR DECADES.**

**BUDGET: £–£££**

Sangiovese goes back a long way to the Romans and their winemaking, with the first official record made in an essay dating from 1600. Sangiovese is by far the most planted black variety in Italy. The best expression of it comes from Tuscany and Chianti is the most famous and successful appellation that uses Sangiovese. It is an adaptable grape: depending upon the terroir and winemaking techniques, the wines can be light and fruit-forward or full-bodied with complexity, but all have a good amount of acidity and tannins. In the 1970s, a group of pioneering winemakers started what became known as the Super Tuscan revolution, blending Sangiovese with international grapes, such as Cabernet Sauvignon and Merlot.

**STYLES:**
Traditional wines will be made of 100 per cent Sangiovese or Sangiovese dominant. These wines have flavours of bitter cherry, herbaceous notes and violets. If aged in new oak, the wines will have great ageing potential, with notes from the oak including vanilla and spice. The Super Tuscan style will also have Sangiovese in the blend but they will have a significant amount of international grape varieties, leading with notes of blackcurrant and black plum.

**FLAVOURS:**
Cherry, raspberry, black plum, black cherry, blackcurrant, herbs, tomatoes, tea

# SOPAIPILLAS
## [PUMPKIN FRITTERS]

**SERVES: 4–6**

——

**TIME: 40 MINS**

——

**VEGETARIAN**

——

500g plain flour, plus extra
  for dusting
250g pumpkin purée
4 tbsp butter, melted
2 tsp baking powder
1 tsp salt
2 tbsp sunflower oil
Pebre (see page 127),
  to serve

*Sopaipillas*, another street food delicacy from Chile, are popular all-year round and are often eaten as an afternoon snack. The pumpkin purée adds a touch of delicious sweetness. My favourite way to serve *sopaipillas* is with my spicy sauce, pebre, but they could also be eaten as a sweet by drizzling with honey or dusting with cinnamon sugar. Try this savoury version with a glass of **Sangiovese**. These wines are very juicy with an abundance of cherry fruits that balance nicely with the slightly sweet character of the *sopaipillas*.

1. Put all the ingredients, except the oil, into a large mixing bowl and mix until a dough is formed. Place the dough on a work surface and knead until you have a smooth dough with a uniform consistency – it will take a good 10 minutes or so. Cover the dough with a damp tea towel and let it rest for 15 minutes.

2. Sprinkle some flour on your work surface or over a large board. Roll out your dough with a rolling pin until it is 0.5cm thick. Use an 8–10cm round cutter to cut out discs – you should be able to make about 15; these are your sopaipillas.

3. Heat the oil in a large non-stick frying pan over a medium heat. Fry the fritters for 3 minutes on each side until they are a golden-brown colour. You may need to cook them in batches, depending on the size of your pan. Once cooked, remove them from the pan and place on some kitchen towel to absorb the oil.

4. Serve the sopaipillas warm with pebre.

# SYRAH [SHIRAZ]

**HOME COUNTRY: FRANCE**

**OTHER COUNTRIES: ARGENTINA, AUSTRALIA, SPAIN, USA**

**MAIN REGIONS: BAROSSA VALLEY, LANGUEDOC-ROUSSILLON, RHÔNE VALLEY**

**FAMOUS APPELLATIONS: CHÂTEAUNEUF-DU-PAPE, CÔTES DU RHÔNE, CÔTE-RÔTIE, CROZES-HERMITAGE, HERMITAGE, SAINT-JOSEPH**

**SWEETNESS: DRY**

**FRUITS: HIGH**

**ACIDITY: MEDIUM TO HIGH**

**ALCOHOL: MEDIUM TO HIGH**

**TANNINS: MEDIUM**

**BODY: FULL**

**GLASSWARE: RED**

**TEMPERATURE: ROOM**

**CELLAR: 5–20+ YEARS**

**BUDGET: £–£££**

Syrah produces stellar varietal wines, especially notable are those from the northern Rhône. It also produces equally fantastic, but very different, blended wines. In the southern Rhône, it is always part of a blend and its favourite partner is Grenache (Garnacha, see page 134). Syrah is strongly perfumed with a spicy character. With a little time, meaty, leathery notes begin to show. In Australia, the Aussies have made the grape their own by renaming it Shiraz. The variety of wine styles produced in Australia is vast ranging – from light and juicy to big and bold.

**STYLES:**
Made as a varietal wine, Syrah is intensely perfumed, with lots of dark fruits, hints of rosemary, and characteristic notes of spicy meat and leather. When it comes to blended wine, Syrah brings to the mix deep coloured blackberries, spices, leather notes, tannins and acidity. It is not normally the main grape of the blend, but rather its companion; Grenache dominates, adding complexity by way of sweet spice and red fruits.

**FLAVOURS:**
Raspberry, plum, black cherry, blackberry, black pepper, leather, chocolate, tobacco

# BEEF SIRLOIN
# WITH CHIPS

**SERVES: 2**

——

**TIME: 90 MINS**

——

2 x good-quality beef sirloin
   steaks (about 150g each)
3 tbsp olive oil
5 tbsp sunflower oil
4 big potatoes, peeled and
   cut into 1cm chips
1 tbsp butter (optional)
250g cherry tomatoes, halved
a large handful of coriander,
   leaves picked
sea salt and black pepper

This book is packed with vegetarian recipes but sometimes
I crave a good piece of meat – and some wines really call for
it. Simple, but satisfying flavours from the beef and chips pair
exceptionally well with the spices, ripe dark fruits and meaty
character of a **Syrah**.

1. Season the steaks with salt and pepper and rub 1 tbsp of
the olive oil all over to coat well. Leave the steak at room
temperature while doing the next steps.

2. Heat the sunflower oil in a large non-stick frying pan over
a medium heat. Fry the chips for 12–15 minutes, turning
occasionally, until they look golden-brown on the outside
and are soft in the middle. You may need to do this in
batches so you don't overcrowd the pan. Remove the chips
to a baking tray lined with kitchen towel to drain, then
season generously with salt.

3. Next, heat a second frying pan over a high heat until almost
smoking. Place the steak in the centre of the pan and cook
for 3 minutes on each side for a medium steak. Add the
butter, if using, towards the end of the cooking time and
baste the meat with the melted butter to get a richer flavour.

4. Remove the steak from the pan and let it rest for 5 minutes.

5. Put the tomatoes and coriander leaves in a bowl. Add the
remaining 2 tablespoons of olive oil and season with salt.

6. Cut the steak into thick slices and serve with the chips
and salad.

# TEMPRANILLO

**HOME COUNTRY: SPAIN**

**OTHER COUNTRIES: ARGENTINA, PORTUGAL**

**MAIN REGIONS: ALENTEJO, DOURO, NAVARRA, PENEDÈS, RIBERA DEL DUERO, RIOJA, TORO**

**FAMOUS APPELLATIONS: NAVARRA, RIBERA DEL DUERO, RIOJA, TORO**

**SWEETNESS: DRY**

**FRUITS: MEDIUM**

**ACIDITY: MEDIUM TO HIGH**

**ALCOHOL: MEDIUM TO HIGH**

**TANNINS: MEDIUM TO HIGH**

**BODY: MEDIUM TO HIGH**

**GLASSWARE: RED**

**TEMPERATURE: ROOM**

**CELLAR: 5–15+ YEARS**

**BUDGET: £–£££**

Tempranillo is the second most planted black grape variety in Spain after Garnacha (see page 134). Ribera del Duero and Rioja are two of the most famous Spanish regions where this grape really excels. Tempranillo has a real affinity for oak, and so in Spain there is a classification that specifically indicates how much time a wine has spent in oak. A wine classified as 'generico', meaning generic, is not required to spend any time in oak, whereas a Crianza spends a minimum of two years ageing, including one year in oak barrels. Reserva is aged for a minimum of three years, including one year in oak barrels followed by a minimum of 6 months ageing in the bottle, and a Gran Reserva is aged for a minimum of five years, including two years in oak barrels. Ribera del Duero, on the central plateau of northern Spain, with its continental climate and altitudes of almost 1,000 metres, has hot days and cool nights. This helps to maintain acidity while at the same time building complexity of flavour. Further north still, Rioja, which is a much larger region, produces wines of varying profiles from delicate to much deeper, richer wines.

**STYLES:**
In light wines the flavours of Tempranillo lean towards fresh fruits such as cherries and strawberries. Many of these wines are unoaked, easy to drink and should be consumed while they are youthful. The richer wines, with more complex flavours and texture, frequently have some level of oak treatment. These wines are laced with a variety of fruits such as raspberries, blackberries and black cherries, with aromas of vanilla and toast from the oak.

**FLAVOURS:**
Cherry, strawberry, raspberry, plum, cinnamon, vanilla, toast

# TORTILLA DE PATATAS
## [POTATO OMELETTE]

**SERVES: 4**

———

**TIME: 45 MINS**

———

**VEGETARIAN**

5 tbsp olive oil
1 onion, finely sliced
300g waxy potatoes,
   cut into thin slices
6 eggs
a small bunch of flatleaf
   parsley, roughly chopped
sea salt and black pepper

Eggs and potatoes are such important food in our kitchen but sadly, they are frequently seen as poor relatives compared to more fashionable ingredients. The truth is that without them you won't be able to cook lots of recipes, including this classic tortilla. This iconic Spanish dish is a clear example of how great eggs and potatoes can be together. **Tempranillo** grapes produce delicious medium-bodied wines with plum, cherries and elegant toasty notes that pair perfectly with the soft texture and flavours of the tortilla.

1. Heat 3 tablespoons of the oil in a large non-stick frying pan over a medium heat. Add the onion and potatoes, place a lid on the pan and cook gently, stirring occasionally, for around 20–30 minutes until everything is golden and tender.

2. Beat the eggs in a large bowl, then add the parsley and the cooked potatoes and onion. Season with salt and pepper and stir to combine.

3. Heat a 22–24cm diameter frying pan over a medium heat. Add the remaining oil and pour the egg and potato mix into the pan. Let it begin to set and then nudge the edges away from the side of the pan using a spatula.

4. Once the tortilla is almost set through, cover the pan with a large plate and carefully invert the pan to flip the tortilla out on to it. Slide the tortilla back into the pan and cook it on the other side for another 2 minutes.

5. Slide the tortilla out of the pan and cut into wedges to serve.

# TOURIGA NACIONAL

**HOME COUNTRY: PORTUGAL**
—

**OTHER COUNTRIES:
AUSTRALIA, USA**
—

**MAIN REGIONS: DAO,
DOURO**
—

**FAMOUS APPELLATIONS:
DAO, DOURO**
—

**SWEETNESS: DRY**
—

**FRUITS: HIGH**
—

**ACIDITY: MEDIUM TO HIGH**
—

**ALCOHOL: HIGH**
—

**TANNINS: HIGH**
—

**BODY: HIGH**
—

**GLASSWARE: RED**
—

**TEMPERATURE: ROOM**
—

**CELLAR: 5–10 YEARS**
—

**BUDGET: £–££**

Touriga Nacional is an incredible versatile grape that produces table wines – dry wines – both as a varietal or as part of a blend. It is also an extremely important component in making Port, a sweet fortified wine (see page 192). Considered to be one of the best black grapes grown in Portugal, its wines are deep in colour and pack an abundance of alcohol and tannin. Perhaps not for the faint-hearted, it's a powerful wine with loads of dark fruits, violets and heady aromas of leather.

**STYLES:**
Varietal wines are powerful with their masculine dark fruits, abundance of tannins, body and richness. In a blended wine, Touriga Nacional adds tannins, alcohol and a complexity of aromas to produce rich, full bodied, balanced wine.

**FLAVOURS:**
Black plum, black cherry, blueberry, black pepper, violet, leather, toast

# FEIJOADA
## [BLACK BEAN STEW]

**SERVES: 4**

—

**TIME: 45 MINS**

—

2 tbsp olive oil
1 onion, roughly chopped
125g pancetta, diced
200g chorizo, diced
2 garlic cloves, crushed
400g tin of black beans
200g salt beef, diced
250ml chicken stock
2 bay leaves
1 tsp dried oregano
a handful of coriander, finely
   chopped
sea salt and black pepper
cooked basmati rice, to serve

Feijoada is the national dish of Brazil. This hearty stew has a mix of meats, giving it complex flavours. It makes a fabulous main for a weekend lunch. Not only is it delicious, but it works well to prepare a day ahead because it tastes even better once the flavours have had time to develop. The powerful flavours of feijoada pair well with the equally potent **Touriga Nacional**.

1. Heat the oil in a large saucepan over a medium heat. Add the onion and cook for 10 minutes until soft and golden in colour.

2. Add the pancetta and chorizo. Cook for around 5 minutes until they are picking up some colour.

3. Next add the garlic, stir and allow to cook for 1 minute before adding the black beans.

4. Add the salt beef, chicken stock, bay leaves and oregano, and season with salt and pepper.

5. Bring the stew to the boil, then reduce the heat to low and simmer for 25 minutes, stirring occasionally.

6. Ladle the stew into bowls and top with a sprinkle of coriander. Serve with freshly cooked basmati rice.

'Not for the faint-hearted, Touriga Nacional is a powerful wine with loads of dark fruits, violets and heady aromas of leather'

TOURIGA NACIONAL WITH FEIJOADA

# SWEET WINE

# SWEET RIESLING

**HOME COUNTRY: GERMANY**

**MAIN REGIONS: MOSEL, PFALZ, RHEINGAU, RHEINHESSEN AND OTHERS**

**FAMOUS APPELLATIONS: MOSEL, PFALZ, RHEINGAU, RHEINHESSEN AND OTHERS**

**SWEETNESS: SWEET**

**FRUITS: HIGH**

**ACIDITY: HIGH**

**ALCOHOL: LOW**

**BODY: FULL**

**GLASSWARE: SMALL GLASS**

**TEMPERATURE: WELL CHILLED**

**CELLAR: 15–20+ YEARS**

**BUDGET: £££**

Riesling is an aromatic grape variety with astonishingly versatility. With its natural high acidity and complex aromas, it produces some extremely long-lived sweet wines. Riesling, like Semillon (see page 180), is susceptible to *Botrytis cinerea* (noble rot, see page 197), which allows the wines to develop flavours of dried apricot, rye bread and honey. Amazing sweet wines are also made from frozen grapes grown in cooler parts of Europe, notably Germany, and, especially, Canada. So-called Eiswein or ice wines display pure and intense fruits and floral aromas. The grapes are left on the vines until the winter, in order to concentrate the flavours and aromas, and then picked and pressed while still frozen to extract the extremely concentrated juice – this is fermented to create an outstanding sweet wine.

**STYLES:**
There are three styles of German Riesling produced with grapes that have been affected by noble rot: Auslese is lightly sweet and has intense dried peach, pineapple and honey flavours; Beerenauslese is characterised as sweet and floral with notes of orange peel and honey; Trockenbeerenauslese is even sweeter than Beerenauslese, but has a similar taste profile. Eiswein, as the name would indicate, is made from frozen grapes. Here the pure flavours of Riesling are present.

**FLAVOURS:**
Lemon, dried apricot, rye bread, orange, pineapple, honey, floral notes

# PANCAKES WITH DULCE DE LECHE

**SERVES: 6**

---

**TIME: 30 MINS**

---

**VEGETARIAN**

---

150g flour
300ml whole milk
2 eggs, beaten
sunflower oil, for frying
500g dulce de leche
　(caramel sauce)
sea salt

This recipe brings back great memories from my childhood. I asked my mom to make pancakes with caramel sauce for breakfast nearly every weekend. I loved them and I still do. Try them yourself and you will know why! Best of all, you can enjoy this recipe for brunch, an afternoon snack or even after a meal! The dulce de leche is delicious with the apricot, orange and rye bread notes in a sweet **Riesling**.

1. Put the flour and a pinch of salt in a large bowl and make a well in the centre.

2. Add the milk and eggs to the well and slowly whisk in, bringing in flour from the edges as you go. Continue whisking until you have a smooth batter without any lumps of flour.

3. Heat a non-stick frying pan over a medium heat and add just a touch of oil.

4. When the pan is hot, add just enough batter to cover the base of the pan, spreading it out over the base by swirling the pan. Cook for 1–2 minutes, until the edges start to crisp up and you see air bubbles on the surface of the pancake. Use a spatula to flip the pancake and cook for another 1 minute on the other side.

5. Place your pancake on a plate. Spread over some of the dulce de leche and roll it up.

6. Repeat to make more pancakes until you've used all of the batter. Drizzle the rolled pancakes with a touch more dulce de leche to serve.

# SAUTERNES

**HOME COUNTRY: FRANCE**

**MAIN REGIONS: BORDEAUX**

**FAMOUS APPELLATIONS: SAUTERNES**

**SWEETNESS: SWEET**

**FRUITS: HIGH**

**ACIDITY: HIGH**

**ALCOHOL: MEDIUM**

**BODY: FULL**

**GLASSWARE: SMALL GLASS**

**TEMPERATURE: WELL CHILLED**

**CELLAR: 10-20+ YEARS**

**BUDGET: £££**

Sauternes is a region in the Graves district of Bordeaux in France, devoted to growing white grapes that are susceptible to a welcome type of fungus that is required to make this style of sweet wine. The region's eponymous wine is one of the most revered sweet wines in the world. All grapes must be harvested by hand, ensuring that each grape picked has been affected by noble rot, and has reached the most advanced stage of rot possible. To achieve this, several passes are made of the vineyards during harvest to select individual grapes as they are ready. Grapes affected by noble rot have a high concentration of sugars and flavours. The fungus (*Botrytis cinerea*) also produces unique flavours such as honey, dried apricot, rye bread and orange marmalade. Although intensely sweet, these wines are balanced with very high acidity, making them one of the most delicious wines in the world.

**GRAPES:**
Sauternes is dominated by Semillon and complemented by a dose of Sauvignon Blanc. Semillon lends body and tropical fruit flavours while Sauvignon Blanc contributes its natural, all-important, high acidity and citrus notes. Muscadelle is sometimes used in small amounts to add texture and floral aromas.

**STYLES:**
Light styles of Sauternes have elegant and delicate fruits, great refreshing acidity and amazing drinkability. Complex versions give intense fruit character, outstanding acidity and a long finish.

**FLAVOURS:**
Lemon, orange peel, dried apricot, rye bread, honey, pineapple

# APRICOTS STUFFED WITH KAYMAK

**SERVES: 4**

———

**TIME: 45 MINS**

———

**VEGETARIAN**

———

5 tbsp sugar
1 vanilla pod, split lengthways
1 cinnamon stick
1 tsp cardamom pods, crushed
zest and juice of ½ lemon
250g dried apricots
  (20–25 pieces)
250g clotted cream
30g pistachios, toasted and
  crushed
30g flaked almonds, toasted
  and crushed
30g walnuts, toasted and
  crushed

The first time I visited Istanbul I was totally enchanted. It was like entering a completely different world. I can still remember the aromas of the Grand Bazaar, the music, the people and of course, the food! Turkish cuisine is vibrant and rich with an immense variety of ingredients and spices. *Kaymak*, or clotted cream, is used in many desserts in Turkey. The intensity of honeyed apricot and citrus flavours of the **Sauternes** are matched by the dried fruits, spices and nuts in this decadent dessert.

1. Put the sugar and 400ml water in a large saucepan, set over a medium heat and stir until all the sugar has dissolved. Add the vanilla pod, cinnamon, cardamom and lemon juice and simmer for 10 minutes.

2. Reduce the heat to low and add the apricots to the pan. Gently poach the apricots in the flavoured sugar syrup for 20 minutes or so until plump. Remove the pan from the heat and allow the apricots to cool in the syrup.

3. Cut each apricot open along the seam to make a little pocket and fill with a teaspoon of clotted cream. Once filled, place on a serving dish and sprinkle the apricots with the pistachios, almonds and walnuts and finally the lemon zest to serve.

'The intensity of honeyed apricot and citrus flavours of the Sauternes are matched by the dried fruits, spices and nuts in this decadent dessert'

SAUTERNES & APRICOTS STUFFED WITH KAYMAK

# TOKAJI

**HOME COUNTRY: HUNGARY**

**MAIN REGIONS: TOKAJI**

**FAMOUS APPELLATIONS: TOKAJI**

**SWEETNESS: DRY TO SWEET**

**FRUITS: HIGH**

**ACIDITY: HIGH**

**ALCOHOL: MEDIUM**

**BODY: FULL**

**GLASSWARE: SMALL GLASS**

**TEMPERATURE: WELL CHILLED**

**CELLAR: 10–20+ YEARS**

**BUDGET: £££**

Tokaji is a famous sweet wine from Hungary made with indigenous grapes. Like French Sauternes and German Sweet Riesling, it is produced from grapes that have been affected by a fungus called *Botrytis cinerea* or noble rot. This fungus grows on the berries, dehydrating them and concentrating sugars. It creates distinctive flavours while maintaining the grape's natural acidity. The wines are aged for long periods of time in new oak barrels before being released.

**GRAPES:**
Furmint is a grape with natural high acidity and flavours of apricot and marzipan. Hárslevelű adds spices, smoke, honey and elderflower to the wine. Sarga Muskotaly is an aromatic variety that contributes additional flavours of melon and grapes.

**STYLES:**
Dry styles represent half of the total production of Tokaji. These wines have a mineral character, great complexity and good ageing potential. Aszú is one the world's most famous sweet wines made from Aszú grapes, meaning ones that have been affected by noble rot. These wines have an intense fruit character and refreshing acidity. Eszencia, also called Nectar, is a very rare style with only 5–6 per cent alcohol and around 450 grams of sugar per litre. These wines have extremely high acidity that, combined with an exceptionally high sugar content, means they have the potential to be stored for centuries!

**FLAVOURS:**
Lemon, orange, mango, pineapple, dried apricot, rye bread, honey

# MOTE CON HUESILLOS
## [CHILEAN BOILED WHEAT WITH DRIED PEACHES]

**SERVES: 6**

———

**TIME: 45 MINUTES, PLUS OVERNIGHT SOAKING**

———

**VEGETARIAN**

250g dried peaches
1 cinnamon stick
1 orange, peel only
500g wheat grain
250g sugar

This is likely the most popular snack in Chile, where, during the spring and summer months, you're never far from a street stand selling *mote con huesillos*. Made with dried peaches and wheat grain, it's a perfect, refreshing snack during the heat of summer. The subtleness of the wheat flavour provides the perfect backdrop to the punch of sweet fruits. The natural high acidity and sweetness of **Tokaji** is a good pairing with this dish.

1. The day before serving, place the dried peaches in a bowl with 250ml water, and add the cinnamon and orange peel. Leave to soak overnight.

2. The next day, cook the wheat in boiling water for 20 minutes, or until tender but still with a little bite to it. Drain and set it aside to cool.

3. Put 125g of the sugar in a saucepan over a medium heat. Allow it to melt and then caramelise, taking the pan off the heat when it becomes golden brown.

4. Slowly, add the soaking water from the peaches, stirring constantly; be careful as it will spit and sizzle. Add the remaining sugar, the peaches, cinnamon and orange peel, put the pan back over a low heat and simmer for 15 minutes.

5. Transfer the mixture to a large container and add the cooked wheat. Allow it to cool completely.

6. Cover the container with a lid and put it in the fridge for at least 30 minutes. Serve cold.

# FORTIFIED WINE

# JEREZ [SHERRY]

**HOME COUNTRY: SPAIN**

**MAIN REGIONS: JEREZ DE LA FRONTERA, PUERTO DE SANTA MARIA, SANLÚCAR DE BARRAMEDA**

**FAMOUS APPELLATIONS: JEREZ DE LA FRONTERA, PUERTO DE SANTA MARIA, SANLÚCAR DE BARRAMEDA**

**SWEETNESS: DRY AND SWEET**

**FRUITS: MEDIUM**

**ACIDITY: MEDIUM**

**ALCOHOL: HIGH**

**BODY: FULL**

**GLASSWARE: SMALL GLASS**

**TEMPERATURE: WELL CHILLED**

**CELLAR: VERY LONG CELLAR LIFE**

**BUDGET: £-££**

**FLAVOURS:**
Lemon, lime, roasted nuts, kernel, almonds, bread, salt, fig, caramel

The southern region of Andalusia in Spain has a long history of producing the fortified wine, Jerez (sherry). Fortified wine is made by boosting the amount of alcohol with the addition of a distilled grape spirit. For Jerez, fortification occurs after alcoholic fermentation is complete. A unique ageing process, known as the solera system, is used to mature and blend the wines. The different styles of Jerez are determined based on the length and type of maturation.

**GRAPES:**
The Palomino grape is used to produce all styles of dry Jerez. It is a neutral grape with relatively low acidity. Pedro Ximénez (PX) is a grape used to create seriously sweet wines. Prior to vinification, the grapes are dried in the sun to concentrate sugars and flavours. PX can also be added to other styles of Jerez to produce sweet sherry. Moscatel of Alexandria is a grape used for blending to add complexity, especially notes of caramel and toffee.

**SOLERA SYSTEM:**
This system of maturation is unique to this region. The wines are aged and blended in a series of large individual casks. It's easiest to think of the casks as forming a pyramid where the youngest wines are introduced at the top and the wine in the bottom casks is ready for bottling. As wine is taken from the oldest casks (never more than about 30 per cent), it is replaced with wine from the above barrels. Old and young wines are blended in a continuous process that results in a consistent style of wine.

**STYLES:**
Fino is pale in colour, light-bodied, salty and citrusy. Manzanilla is a similar style to Fino with a very distinctive salty note. This wine is made in the appellation of Sanlúcar de Barrameda. Amontillado is amber coloured, medium-bodied with a nutty character. For this style, the wine starts as fino and then additional alcohol is added to kill the flor and oxidise the wine. Oloroso is aged without any flor, creating an oxidised wine which is deep brown, highly aromatic and full-bodied. It is characterised by flavours of coffee, dried fruits and roasted nuts.

# SPANISH TAPAS

**SERVES: 4**

—

**TIME: 10 MINS**

—

200g jamón Serrano,
  thinly sliced
200g Manchego, sliced
200g Manzanilla olives
200g boquerones (fresh
  marinated anchovies)
200g dulce de membrillo
  (quince paste)
5 tbsp extra virgin olive oil
a loaf of rustic bread,
  warmed, to serve

Here is a suggestion for putting together your own tapas assortment at home. The key is to buy excellent quality ingredients. One of the things that makes tapas so enjoyable is the small portions, which allow you to taste several dishes with different flavours and textures. Salty foods such as these are a great match for nearly any wine. The salt enhances the wine, making it seem fruitier and smoother. **Jerez** is the natural pairing with tapas. There are several styles that are worth trying as each has its own personality.

1. Arrange all the ingredients in your own way, using small plates, bowls or boards. They should be at room temperature and not directly from the fridge.

2. Serve with warm bread.

# PORT

**HOME COUNTRY: PORTUGAL**

---

**MAIN REGIONS: DOURO**

---

**FAMOUS APPELLATIONS: DOURO**

---

**SWEETNESS: SWEET**

---

**FRUITS: HIGH**

---

**ACIDITY: MEDIUM**

---

**ALCOHOL: HIGH**

---

**BODY: FULL**

---

**GLASSWARE: SMALL GLASS**

---

**TEMPERATURE: ROOM**

---

**CELLAR: YOUNG STYLES ARE READY TO BE CONSUMED. VINTAGE PORTS CAN AGE FOREVER.**

---

**BUDGET: £-£££**

---

**FLAVOURS:**
Cherry, strawberry, blueberry, blackberry, toffee, caramel, dried fruits

It's not clear exactly when the first Port wine was made. According to legend, a couple of wine merchants visiting the Douro Valley in Portugal came across the Abbot of Lamego while he was halting fermentation of wine by the addition of grape spirit. When the fermentation is interrupted in this fashion, not all of the sugar in the wine has had time to be converted to alcohol and the resulting wine is sweet. Regardless of how it was discovered, fortification was important because it allowed the wines to successfully travel from the Douro to Porto on the coast, and on to England, without spoilage. It also creates a wine that is capable of ageing for decades.

**GRAPES:**
Touriga Nacional is the most famous of all varieties and creates dark wines with high concentration of fruits and tannins. Touriga Francesa, the most planted variety in the Douro Valley, adds fresh fruits, a seductive floral component and firm tannins. Tinta Roriz, also known as Tempranillo, produces wines with elegant structure, intense aromas and great ageing potential. Tinta Barroca produces rich and deeply coloured wines with a soft texture and delicate aromas. Tinta Cão, one of the oldest varieties in the region, produces wines with great acidity and a velvety texture. White Port is made with different grapes, such as Malvasia Fina, Gouveio and Rabigato.

**STYLES:**
White Port is an easy-to-drink wine that is a perfect aperitif. Ruby Ports are youthful and fiery – a powerful style with jammy red fruits. Tawny Port gets its name from its pale brown colour. These Ports possess lighter body and are characterised by their nutty and caramel flavours with cooked berries and toasty oak. Vintage Port is only made in the best vintages and is the most prestigious. These wines can age for a long time and are rich and complex.

# CHOCOLATE BROWNIES

**SERVES: 10**

—

**TIME: 45 MINS**

—

**VEGETARIAN**

—

200g unsalted butter,
    plus extra for greasing
200g dark chocolate chips
175g caster sugar
3 eggs
30g cocoa powder
75g plain flour
1 tsp vanilla extract

There can be few people in the world who don't love chocolate. Why not indulge that craving with something really rich and chocolatey? In Portugal, **Port** is commonly served as an aperitif. In most other places, it is drunk on its own after the meal or paired with dessert. Port's powerful profile requires a dessert equally rich so as not to be overwhelmed. Here is the perfect recipe!

1. Preheat the oven to 180°C/gas 4. Grease and line a 20cm square baking tin with baking paper.

2. Place the butter and chocolate chips in a heatproof glass bowl set over a saucepan with a couple of centimetres of barely simmering water and melt, stirring occasionally.

3. Remove the bowl from the saucepan and allow the chocolate to cool slightly. Add the sugar and combine, then the eggs, beating in before adding the cocoa, flour and vanilla. Give it one final mix until the flour is just incorporated, being careful not to overmix.

4. Pour the batter into the lined tin. Bake for around 25–30 minutes until the edges are set and the centre is fudgy.

5. Leave in the tin to cool completely before cutting.

# GLOSSARY

**ACIDITY** – Every wine has some amount of acidity. You can best detect acidity on your tongue – it's a tingling sensation. The presence of acidity makes your mouth water.

**ALCOHOL** – The amount of alcohol in a wine is part of what gives wine its body. Wines below 11 per cent are considered low in alcohol. Above 14 per cent wines are high in alcohol.

**ALCOHOLIC FERMENTATION** – The process by which the sugar in grape juice is converted to alcohol with the addition of yeast.

**AOC** (Appellation d'Origine Contrôlée – Protected Designation of Origin) – A classification found on French wine labels indicating a high level of quality. In order to earn this classification, producers must adhere to all of the rules/ laws of their given region that define the approved growing area, aspects of grape growing and winemaking.

**AOP** (Appellation d'Origine Protégée) – The current appellation system that regulates the production of wine in France. This system replaced the previous AOC (Appellation d'Origine Contrôlée) in 2012.

**APPASSIMENTO TECHNIQUE** – A winemaking technique where ripe grapes are harvested and then air-dried prior to being used to make wine.

**APPELLATION** – A defined wine area. Within Europe these areas have a set of rules and/or laws that regulate what type of grapes are grown and the type(s) of wine made.

**AROMATIC GRAPE VARIETIES** – Usually referring to white varieties, these grapes give off an extremely high volume of natural aromas.

**BARRIQUE** – Refers to a specific type of small oak barrel that can impart notes to the wine such as toast or vanilla if they are new (on their first use).

**BLEND** – A wine made from more than one grape variety. A blend can also be the same variety but from different vintages to make a house blend, as is the case with champagne and fortified wines.

**BODY** – The sensation of how a wine feels in the mouth. Many things contribute to the body of wine, including tannins, alcohol and residual sugar.

**BORDEAUX BLEND** – A typical combination of grapes grown in the region to create a distinctive style of wine. This adds complexity, because the distinctive attributes of each variety contribute to the wine. For reds, the classic combination is Cabernet Sauvignon, Merlot and Cabernet Franc. For whites, the blend is Semillon, Sauvignon Blanc, Muscadelle and a little Sauvignon Gris.

**BOTRYTIS CINEREA** – Also known as 'noble rot', *Botrytis cinerea* is a fungus that attacks healthy grapes. The fungus breaks the skin of grapes allowing the water to evaporate from the berries, concentrating the sugar while retaining great acidity. Botrytised grapes are used to make sweet wines.

**CARBONIC MACERATION** – A winemaking technique in which whole bunches of grapes are fermented, allowing most of the juice within the berry to ferment before they are crushed. This technique produces wines that will have light body, low tannins and intense red fruit character.

**CLASSICO** – Found on Italian wine labels, the term indicates wines that come from close to the historic centre. These vineyards are generally found on slopes and are usually the best and oldest vineyards in the region.

**COMPLEX WINE/COMPLEXITY** – Describes a wine that has many flavours that reveal themselves during the process of tasting.

**CRU** – A French term denoting that a particular producer, village or vineyard has met specific qualifications that allow the use of that term, depending on the region in which the wine has been produced.

**CRUSHING** – Gently breaking the wine skins to release some of the grape juice.

**DOC** (Denominazione di Origine Controllata – Denomination of Controlled Origin) / **DOCG** (Denominazione di Origine Controllata e Garantita – Denomination of Controlled and Guaranteed Origin) – Classifications found on Italian wine labels indicating a high level of quality. In order to earn this classification producers must adhere to all of the rules/laws of their given region that define the approved growing area, aspects of grape growing and winemaking. DOCG is the highest level of classification within Italy.

**DO** (Denominación de Origen – Designation of Origin) / **DOCa** (Denominación de Origen Calificada – Qualified Designation of Origin) – Classifications found on Spanish wine labels indicating a high level of quality. In order to earn this classification producers must adhere to all of the rules/laws of their given region that define the approved growing area, aspects of grape growing and winemaking. Regions that are designated DO indicate that this is a quality-controlled appellation. DOCa is a more prestigious classification, requiring the most stringent quality criteria.

**DRY** (wine) – The absence of noticeable residual sugar with a maximum limit of 4 grams of sugar per litre.

**FLOR** – A thin layer of yeast that forms on top of Jerez wines in the casks. The flor prevents oxygen from reaching the wine.

**FORTIFIED WINE** – A wine that has had additional neutral grape spirit added to it. The addition can be made during or after fermentation.

**HARVEST** – The act of picking the ripe grapes from the vines.

**LEES** – Dead yeast cells that remain after fermentation.

**LEES STIRRING/CONTACT** – A winemaker may choose to keep the dead yeast cells (lees) in the wine. The contact with the lees adds texture and flavour to the wine.

**MADEIRA** – A fortified wine from the Portuguese island of Madeira. This wine has an amber colour and a distinctive flavour that derives from repeatedly heating it.

**MATURATION** – The act of leaving a finished wine to rest/mature in bottle or maturation vessel (for example, an oak barrel).

**NEUTRAL GRAPE** – A grape that has relatively simple flavours, dominated by the citrus flavours of lemon and lime. Several grape varieties are neutral in flavour, among them Pinot Grigio, Ugni Blanc and Palomino. They can make wines that are neutral in their own right or can add their neutral character to a blend.

**NOBLE ROT** – A benevolent type of fungus – see *Botrytis cinerea*.

**NON-VINTAGE** – A wine that is made from a blend of wines from different vintages (years).

**NOSE** – The aromas that are detected when smelling a wine.

**OAKED** – When a wine is placed in a (new/old) oak barrel for fermentation and/or ageing. The vanillins – organic compounds – present in the oak are responsible for adding flavour (subtly or strongly) to wines such as Chardonnay in Burgundy, Tempranillo in Rioja and other wines from around the world.

**OFF DRY** (wine) – The presence of residual sugar with a maximum limit of 12 grams of sugar per litre.

**OXIDATION** – A wine fault caused by a chemical reaction as a result of wine being exposed to oxygen during the winemaking process or after bottling.

**PALATE** – The various tastes and sensations you get when tasting a wine.

**PHYLLOXERA** – An aphid pest, *Phylloxera vastatrix*, that destroys grape vines by attacking their roots, eventually leading to the death of the vine.

**RESIDUAL SUGAR** – Sugar that remains in the finished wine after fermentation is complete.

**SECONDARY FERMENTATION** – Fermenting a still wine in a new vessel by the addition of yeast and sugar. This is normally how sparkling wine is made.

**SÉLECTION DE GRAINS NOBLES** – A style of sweet wine made from grapes affected by noble rot. This is the top classification for sweet wines in the region of Alsace.

**SKIN CONTACT** – A stage during the winemaking process, also known as 'maceration'. The skins from the grapes will be in contact with the juice in the fermentation vessel for a specific period of time in order to increase the flavours, body and/or tannins. Skin contact is very popular in red wine production because it adds colour, tannins and complexity to the wines.

**SUPER TUSCAN** – A premium style of red wine produced in the region of Tuscany in Italy using indigenous varieties, such as Sangiovese, with the addition of international varieties, for example Cabernet Sauvignon and Merlot.

**SWEET WINE** – A wine that has residual sugar left in the finished wine.

**TANK METHOD** – A method for creating sparkling wine using a large stainless-steel tank under pressure. See also traditional method.

**TANNIN** – Tannins come from the skins of grapes and cause the inside of your mouth to feel dry. They are generally found in red wines. Their presence enables red wines to age, sometimes for decades.

**TERROIR** – The environment in which grapevines are grown. This encompasses the soil, climate and topography but also includes human factors, such as the orientation of the vines, irrigation, pruning and vine-training systems.

**TRADITIONAL METHOD** – The term used to describe the process for making Champagne and other bottle-fermented sparkling wines. Several stages are needed to create a sparkling wine using the traditional method:

- *Liqueur de tirage* – this refers to a solution of sugar, wine and yeast that is added to the base wine to start the secondary fermentation in the bottle.

- Riddling – after the ageing period, the bottles are tilted and rotated to ensure the yeast sediment collects in the neck of the bottle.

- Disgorgement – the removal of the dead yeast (lees) from the bottle.

- Dosage – the addition of a small amount of *liqueur d'expédition* (sugar and wine) to balance the acidity and determine how sweet the sparkling wine will be.

**UNOAKED** – A wine that does not spend any time in oak barrels during maturation and ageing.

**VARIETAL** – A wine made from only a single grape variety.

**VENDANGE TARDIVE** ('late harvest') – A style of sweet wine made in the region of Alsace from grapes that have been left on the vine for a longer period of time to concentrate the sugars before harvest.

**VINIFICATION** – The process of fermenting grape juice to produce wine.

**VINTAGE** – The year in which the grapes are harvested.

**YEAST** – A fungus that, when combined with sugar, creates alcohol.

# INDEX

# ACKNOWLEDGEMENTS

I would like to thank to all my students, colleagues and clients from the wine trade who encouraged me to embark on this project. Their support was crucial to start this amazing journey.

I was very lucky to have two amazing collaborators that helped me write this book. Their views and constant feedback were extremely helpful during the writing process. The creative and fun environment enabled good ideas to thrive. To my dear wine friends Sheri Orts and William Randle, thank you.

Thanks to my dream team who worked in such a brilliant way to create the actual book. Sian Henley, a super talented recipe tester and great chef who brought extreme attention to detail in every dish and recipe. Steven Joyce, an amazing photographer that was able to properly reflect my way of cooking with beautiful pictures. Lauren Law, a great prop stylist with a very clear vision and extremely good taste when it came to 'dress' the pictures. Thanks to Grace Paul – assistant Chef – and Tom Groves – assistant photographer.

Big thanks to all the team at whitefox but in particular to George Edgeller for his incredible patience and support with this project.

I would also love to thank a very special group of people who were always there for me during this process: Moravia Pastori, Rebecca Seal, Andrew Fishwick, Martin Fishwick, Tomas Larrain, Helio Andrade, Beatriz Silva, Graham Cox, David Martin, Alex Stevenson, Cristiano Feijo, Cameron McKeown, Giulia Sarti and Ryan Dunn.

Lastly, I want to thank my beautiful family: Silvia Diaz, Raul Herrera, Andres Sandoval, Silvia Solar, Margarita Lopez, Gregoria Muñoz, Ana Diaz, Patricia Diaz, Andrea Diaz, Kiko Diaz, Patricio Herrera, Cristian Herrera, Leonor Herrera, Margarita Herrera, Patricio Nuñez, Jorge Carmona, Carolina Herrera, Pablo and Sebastian Saldivia, Camila, Jose Manuel and Constanza Alruiz, Stephanie Päplow and Andres Solis.

Raul Diaz

First published in 2020 by Merken

ISBN 978-1912892631

Photography: Steven Joyce
Design: Louise Evans
Copyeditor: Becci Woods
Proofreader: Stephanie Evans
Home economist: Sian Henley
Prop stylist: Lauren Law
Project management by whitefox
Printed and bound by Ozgraf